MATT RUBINSTEIN

SOLSTICE

*un*tapped

ABOUT *UNTAPPED*

Most Australian books ever written have fallen out of print and become unavailable for purchase or loan from libraries. This includes important local and national histories, biographies and memoirs, beloved children's titles, and even winners of glittering literary prizes such as the Miles Franklin Literary Award.

Supported by funding from state and territory libraries, philanthropists and the Australian Research Council, *Untapped* is identifying Australia's culturally important lost books, digitising them, and promoting them to new generations of readers. As well as providing access to lost books and a new source of revenue for their writers, the *Untapped* collaboration is supporting new research into the economic value of authors' reversion rights and book promotion by libraries, and the relationship between library lending and digital book sales. The results will feed into public policy discussions about how we can better support Australian authors, readers and culture.

See untapped.org.au for more information, including a full list of project partners and rediscovered books.

Readers are reminded that these books are products of their time. Some may contain language or reflect views that might now be found offensive or inappropriate.

6:00 am

It's early: six, to be exact.
The sky is huge and dark, and filled
with pre-dawn silence; also packed
with points of light. The air is chilled.
The scene: a hill outside of town,
an old reserve where no one goes.
A snaking highway slithers down
where, far below, the city glows.
A sea of white and orange shines
as every vigilant streetlight,
still flicking in the dark, combines
to wrap the earth in tendrils bright.
The view is luminously grand,
as of some neon fairyland.

6:03 am

No fairies live, though, on these streets,
beneath the constant neon buzz.
No sprites reside where asphalt meets
with bitumen—but Arthur does.
A ragged man, with dirt-blond locks
and beard, he calls the street his home.
His castle is a cardboard box;
his bed, a square of packing foam.
A trenchcoat for his regal robe,
a football beanie for a crown,
Art looks like some misfortuned Job,
but is, it's said, the King of Town.
For in this world of buildings tall,
the man who rules the streets, rules all.

6:06 am

Art's sleep is fitful, and possessed
by unknown and tormenting dreams.
His knees tucked up against his chest,
his eyes shut tight, he almost seems
a baby, sleeping on the dirty
cement: his face shows innocence
and fear. But he is almost thirty:
a life concerned with self-defence
and preservation's left him hard.
He's lived alone for all his years,
and knows always to be on guard.
But on his cheeks: could they be tears?
For Arthur's past of anguish deep
is channelled out when he's asleep.

6:09 am

By day, the Sidewalk King is cool.
Man-about-town, he's much admired
by all around, and likes to rule
with thumbless glove. So he's required
to make light of his sad misfortunes.
But in the night he must confront
the shame he hides when he importunes
money from strangers, with a blunt
'A dollar, please, sir—you can spare it!'
So fast asleep, he weeps inside.
Although he knows he shouldn't care, it
still hurts a man with so much pride
to beg. But now, a car-horn's blast
retrieves Art from his painful past.

6:12 am

He stirs, still stiff, and rubs his limbs
to shake the cold of night away.
He tries to rise too fast, and swims
a moment in the Chardonnay
he drank last night. A drop too much,
perhaps, but it's his favourite wine;
a connoisseur would never touch
the methylated turpentine
his brothers on the street imbibe,
and Art's a connoisseur. His head
now clear, he searches out the tribe
of which he is the chieftain: spread
around the city, Arthur's kin
arise, and clutch their bags of gin.

6:15 am

Above the hill, stars start to fade,
then dwindle sadly one by one.
The dark blue takes an orange shade
in preparation for the sun
about to make its longest way
across the sky: it's late December;
the summer solstice is today.
Off to the east, the glowing ember
bursts into flame above the cliff.
Light floods through the abandoned quarry
and gleams off every rock as if
pure gold, instead of shale and sorry
sandstone boulders littered the ground
(occasionally, quartz is found).

6:18 am

The web of light stretched out below
echoes the light above, and starts
to fade; the reassuring glow
of luminescent globes departs.
The major highways are still lit:
some early headlamps limp along.
The airport's runway lights have quit,
and Boeings roar a morning song.
The city slowly wakes and yawns.
A thousand magpies warble cheerful.
Newspapers grace ten thousand lawns;
a million sleepers get an earful
of early morning clock alarms
and breakfast show announcers' charms.

6:21 am

'Good morning, listeners, this is Dean
McLean, and you're on 5AJ.
You just heard "My Best Friend" from Queen,
and there's some Pink Floyd on the way.
Some weather: thirty-five degrees,
no rain. But hey, what else is new?
Could someone get my coffee, please?
It's early. I'm asleep. Aren't you?
Right, how about some music? Fine.
Here's "Dark Side of the Moon". I'm here
each morning until half-past nine.
Hey! It's the summer solstice. We're—'
But Dean McLean is silenced by
an intervention from on high.

6:24 am

Rebecca runs a weary hand
through her short, black—unruly—crop
of hair. She's tall. Her skin is tanned,
eyes green. She works in a bookshop.
Eighteen years old, she studies Arts
at university—except,
of course, she stops when summer starts.
She likes to read. She's quite adept
at tennis, listens to The Cure,
wants to see Chile and Belize
but worries that she won't before
she's too old to enjoy it. She's
a movie buff and film collector:
Hitchcock's her favourite director.

6:27 am

Promotion posters from the master
of film suspense are hung around
the walls. More paper shows than plaster,
from *Secret Agent* to *Spellbound*.
To Catch a Thief and *Rope* adorn
the space above her bed. *The Birds,*
Suspicion, Under Capricorn,
in matte montage, with frantic words:
'Most Terrifying!', 'Grimmest!', 'Best!'
and similar superlatives.
Notorious. North by Northwest.
But special pride of place she gives
the royal gem of her exchequer:
the movie named for her. *Rebecca.*

6:30 am

Rebecca stumbles from her room
and finds the bathroom down the hall.
She seals it, like a welcome tomb,
and hangs her nightshirt on the wall.
Stepping beneath the steaming shower,
she thinks about the day ahead:
so passes almost half an hour.
She wishes she were back in bed,
but as the gently pulsing jets
of water beat upon her skin,
infecting her with warmth, she lets
her body wake. Indiscipline
won't let her leave the shower till
the water heater starts to chill.

6:33 am

The morning's silence has become
a distant memory. A clamour
of discord fills the air: the thrum
of TV sets turned high, the stammer
of starter motors stalling, speeding;
the shrieks of schoolchildren, augmented
by harrowed parents' helpless pleading
and resignation. Discontented
creatures miaow and bark for food;
spin-driers and dishwashers churn.
A radio plays 'In the Mood';
breakfasters curse as crumpets burn.
Bells on the boom-gates down the lane
announce the passing of a train.

6:36 am

Kristin yawns, stretches, rubs her eyes
and blearily stares through the glass
of the train window. Tired, she lies
awkwardly in her second class
reclining seat. Against the odds
she's been asleep for several hours:
the clanking of the wheels, the squads
of restless kids, the drunk who cowers
suspiciously across the aisle—
all have been powerless to keep
her from her rest. Though for a while
she stayed awake and fumed, soon sleep
(that ever-welcome anaesthetic)
left her sublimely apathetic.

6:39 am

Kris comes from Copenhagen, though
few people guess it from her face.
Her dark skin, jet-black hair and doe-
brown eyes suggest another place
much closer to this sunburnt land
than blonde and blue-eyed Scandinavia,
where girls like her comprise a band
apart. But travel's been her saviour:
eleven thousand miles from home,
she left Denmark six months ago,
each cell—each very chromosome—
just yearning to explore, to know
more of the world than her home-town.
Since then, her world's turned upside-down.

6:42 am

She backpacked through the northern lands,
saw fjords from Bergen to Stockholm,
and walked Helsinki's chilly sands
until she felt disposed to roam
across the Baltic Sea, to Russia
(once documents had been arranged,
an exercise she feared would crush her).
Now comprehensively estranged
from homeland, she continued west,
emerging from the Iron Curtain
to Munich for Oktoberfest.
A week or two—she can't be certain—
and then she rode the rails to Rome
and gave no thought to going home.

6:45 am

Six months of travel are a blur;
two hundred days have passed as one.
She sometimes can't believe it's her
adventuring like this. She's done
so much, but missed so much: the world
is small, it's true, but also huge.
She feels as though her life's been hurled
into a giant centrifuge
of tickets, guidebooks, hostels, maps,
bureaux de change, museums, art,
new languages and tourist traps.
It all weighs heavy on her heart
as she arrives, without regalia,
in Adelaide, in South Australia.

6:48 am

A coffee and some cornflakes later,
Rebecca's on the town-bound bus.
The driver flicks an indicator;
a slacker climbs aboard. 'Hey, Gus!'
Rebecca calls; he sits beside her:
'Hey, Bec.' 'That's all you have to say?'
she reprimands her fellow rider:
'I haven't seen you out this way
for weeks!' 'I've been... preoccupied.'
Bec smiles: 'I worried you were ill—
as time went on, I thought you'd died.
But since it seems you're breathing still,
you must be seeing someone new.'
Gus gives a bashful smile: 'It's true.

6:51 am

'We met at work—you know, the bar
I work at: she came in with friends,
I started playing the guitar,
she sang along. That's where it ends.'
'A modern fairytale!' Bec cries.
'And what's your Cinders like, Prince Charming?'
'She's tall, like you. Blonde hair, blue eyes,
nice lips—a smile that's quite disarming.
A sense of humour, and some brains.
She's great.' 'She sounds it.' 'Yes—but now,
how's life with you?' Rebecca feigns
indifference; Gus continues: 'How
is that guy you were seeing when
I saw you last?' Bec winces: 'Glenn.'

6:54 am

Glenn finds himself at once alert—
an hour or two before he'd hoped,
but all his efforts to revert
to dreaming are in vain: unroped
and undirected fragments fly
elusively from consciousness,
and fleeting images defy
articulation. Glenn's success
in sleeping is the stuff of fable:
his friends say he'd doze through a flood.
And so it's odd that he's unable
to dull the prickle in his blood:
the spark that just won't go away
and makes him thirst to taste this day.

6:57 am

His room is large, and full of light:
the floor is spacious and uncluttered.
A double futon dressed in white
and grey reposes by the shuttered
windows. A set of juggling balls
lie in a triad on the floor,
next to the stereo. The walls
were once stark plaster, but no more:
Glenn's cheerfully artistic flair
and disregard for protocol
soon set upon each surface bare
with cans of gleeful aerosol,
transforming it from silent white
into a mural of delight.

7:00 am

One lavish corner may betray
a tendency to the romantic:
here errant knights and knaves display
their chivalry, and sycophantic
courtiers woo indifferent queens,
while good and evil warring nations
do battle in chaotic scenes.
Next comes a mass of scrawled quotations,
like: "Fight the power!" "Smash the state!"
"Increase the peace!" "Preserve the planet!"
"Go somewhere else and procreate!"
"The future is a pomegranate."
Then, "When in doubt, just grin and fake it—
reality is what you make it."

7:03 am

From this melange of aphorism,
Glenn's flowing frieze of sidewalk art
(or post-post-post-impressionism)
dissolves into its final part:
a red and orange sunset, glowing
above a near-deserted beach.
The painted palm trees gently blowing
appear almost to be in reach,
so finely are they rendered. Tracks
of footprints stretch along the shore;
the scene is one of graceful pax
Australiana. But there's more:
before a gold-inflected sea,
Rebecca leans against a tree.

7:06 am

It looks just like her. Tall, dark hair;
Glenn searched for days to find a shade
of green to match her eyes. The glare
of sunset hangs like gold brocade
across her body, decked in silk
that floats, seductive, in the breeze.
She flashes teeth like drops of milk
and gazes through the swaying trees
towards the bedroom. Glenn returns
her stare, remembering the way
she'd pose for him on their sojourns
to summer beaches: every day,
when waking, he beholds his frieze,
and is entranced by what he sees.

7:09 am

'That's right,' says Gus: 'So, how's it going?'
Rebecca hasn't said a word
for several bus stops, and is showing
no sign whatever that she's heard
him now. So he continues: 'Earth
to Becca? This is Ground Control!'
But she's impervious to mirth;
a shadow-smile is all his droll
attempts can bring: 'Oh, sorry, Gus.
I was a thousand miles away.
It's not the best thing to discuss
with me, this morning.' 'You don't say!
But if you need a friendly ear—
someone to talk to—well, I'm here.'

7:12 am

But how can she hope to explain
what she, herself, can't understand?
The rush of doubt and fear of pain
she feels whenever Glenn's at hand,
cruelly tempering the joy
that greets his presence and his touch;
the clashing energies that toy
with her emotions are too much
to deal with, let alone relate.
It would be folly and pretence
to think that talking could placate
the merciless ambivalence
she feels. So she is forced to say:
'I'm sorry, Gus. Perhaps some day.'

7:15 am

Arthur observes the crawling traffic
with half-amused bewilderment.
Excluded from this demographic,
he and his friends are quite content
to take advantage of the streets
built for the automotive age:
now his contingent blithely beats
the system, glad to disengage
and rule the roads that others' taxes
have subsidised, while those poor others
suffer the horror that climaxes
in jams like this. Art and his brothers
have no such trouble with commuting—
and neither are their feet polluting.

7:18 am

He stands among the rush-hour crowd
as in a hurricane's still eye—
for he alone remains unbowed
by hordes of strangers hurtling by,
making a wide but subtle berth
around the slight embarrassment
that Art embodies. With some mirth
he charts the limits of the dent
he's made within the urgent crush:
the only space to pause, without
being uprooted by the rush,
is that small, hallowed space about
the Sidewalk King. He's not offended,
nor was this outcome unintended.

7:21 am

Another eddy in the mass
begins to gravitate toward
Art's haven, carving a crevasse
among the people, yet ignored
by everybody. It's Slow Eddie,
so named because his urban trade
proceeds at such a creeping, steady
tempo: no can of lemonade,
emptied and hurled into a bin,
was ever fetched with so much care
as Ed endows each wayward tin.
An artisan without compare,
his seemingly deranged obsession
creates an art of his profession.

7:24 am

'You won't believe what I just found,'
he gushes as he reaches Art.
'A Mello Yello Melon! Round
these parts they're pretty rare. Apart
from scratches, it's in perfect mint
condition. It's an import, see:
ingredients in different print
from local cans. No guarantee
I'll find another in a hurry.
The rest is mostly Coke—some Diet,
some caffeine-free. You know, I worry
about this stuff. Not game to try it!
No sugar? No caffeine? Bereft
of these, just fizzy water's left.'

7:27 am

As Kristin drains the final drops
of cola from her can, she gives
no second thought to he who swaps
such treasures for hard cash, who lives
by dint of what she now discards.
Her interrupted sleep is weighing
heavily on her now; the shards
of sunlight needle her, delaying
all secondary thought until
she's found a place to call her home,
to rest a moment and refill
her stores of energy. To roam
incessantly is always tiring:
the thought of shelter, thus, inspiring.

7:30 am

Labouring tortoise-like beneath
her backpack, Kristin slowly makes
her way across a shady wreath
of parkland. Weary joy awakes
as she beholds a painted sign:
the cosy hut and crooked tree
that universally define,
from Timbuktu to Tennessee,
the nearby presence of a hostel
somewhere around the neighbourhood.
Her joy is almost pentecostal:
it lifts her step and does her good
to contemplate the spartan bed
that lies a minute's walk ahead.

7:33 am

There's one or more in every town,
in every place where people go.
From four-star inn to tumble-down
old cottage, castle in the snow
to redefined Olympic quarters,
the hospitable hostel lends
asylum to all pilgrims. Porters
are rare; no chambermaid attends
the dormitory rooms that sleep
eight travellers or more; but, sparse
and functional, these rooms are cheap,
and most, in atmosphere, outclass
the finest Ritz hotel: each dorm
is friendly, sociable, and warm.

7:36 am

Expending her conclusive ounce
of energy, Kris heaves her pack
onto a bunk bed to announce
her new dominion. Lying back,
she breathes a sigh of pure relief,
as of a tankless diver rising
after a plunge below a reef,
gasping for air. It's not surprising
that hostels have this glad effect
on Kris: away from home and friends,
they serve to nurture and protect
against the unknown. She depends
on constants in this world arcane:
she clings to them; they keep her sane.

7:39 am

Across town, in another lonely
hotel room, Zoe, deep in thought,
paces a well-worn path. The only
completed part of her report,
which gazes with contempt and scorn
from inside her computer screen,
contains the working title: 'Dawn
To After Dusk: The Tourist Scene
In Quite Exciting Adelaide',
and she's not even sure of that.
Zoe's a journalist by trade,
a *New York Times* aristocrat
famous for her excoriations
of once-proud cities, states and nations.

7:42 am

Brandishing her expense account,
she's stayed in all the finest places,
sampled a mountainous amount
of food, seen triumphs and disgraces
of theatre, cinema and art,
evaluated atmosphere.
A literary Bonaparte,
she tramples all she chances near,
wielding a lethal word processor
far mightier than any sword.
An unappeasable assessor,
alternately esteemed and awed,
she's known for her infrequent mercy,
but more so for her controversy.

7:45 am

She found that Switzerland was 'boring,
with far too many clocks'. The Louvre
was 'cluttered, dark, and underawing',
and she could only disapprove
of Venice, 'wet and overrated'.
The Hermitage was 'badly planned',
the Eiffel Tower, 'sadly dated...
too pricey'. On the other hand,
she liked the Skansen Park in Sweden,
admired the food in Kathmandu,
thought India 'a second Eden',
and didn't want to leave Peru.
Her constancy is non-existent:
she's uniformly inconsistent.

7:48 am

This morning's bout of critic's block
is something that she's never known:
since starting work at six o'clock,
her desperation's slowly grown
until, two bitter hours later,
eleven words of paltry title
reflect the woe of their creator.
Such industry without requital
is unfamiliar to Zo:
her thoughts are all in disarray,
sentences seize, and words won't flow.
She doesn't know quite what to say
about this enigmatic town
of wholly indistinct renown.

7:51 am

For, after having spent two days
in search of things to scrutinise,
she's not composed a single phrase.
Her tendency to criticise
can find no object for its wrath:
no lavishly portrayed pretensions
to savage like an Ostrogoth,
no pitiful misapprehensions
of ostentation to correct—
the place seems humble, unassuming
and inoffensive. The effect
of this reserve has Zoe fuming:
she longs to know the secret pride
this city seems content to hide.

7:54 am

The hair that hangs in Zoe's eyes
is red. The eyes themselves are green,
enthusiastic, searching, wise.
Her skin is pale. She's svelte and lean.
She's getting close to twenty-six,
but doesn't think that old age comes
till thirty-eight. A string of tricks
removed her from the high-class slums
of New York's suburbs, years ago,
and landed her the dream job which
has brought her to this impasse. Zo,
despite her lifestyle, isn't rich:
she trails the dictates of her will,
and other people foot the bill.

7:57 am

After a brief but final pause,
she vengefully kills her computer,
slowly descends through fourteen floors,
ignores a lobby collocutor,
asks for her mail, hands in her keys
and checks out for the day. Her goal
is strengthened by her fury: she's
intent to learn, and so extol
or damn, the secrets of the city.
Should she expire in the attempt,
her death would surely be a pity,
but nothing other will pre-empt
her satisfaction. Heart and feet
resolved, she sets out on the street.

8:00 am

The city breathes a sigh of solace
as morning rush hour slowly dwindles.
The working masses of the polis
are now engaged in sales and swindles,
ensconced in dazzling mirrored towers,
vertiginously overlooking
the warming streets below. Eight hours
a day, they are preserved from cooking
beneath the sun by tireless air
conditioning, a luxury
excluded from the savoir-faire
of ancient Icarus, when he
ambitiously resolved to rise
analogously to the skies.

8:03 am

Rebecca's haunt is far below
these castles of a modern age,
whose turrets, in a faceless row
of gentle apricot and beige,
demand a tribute of respect.
But Magnum Opus, bookshop for
the people, doesn't genuflect
before these spires of glass and awe.
A proud and angry Lilliputian
between the feet of concrete giants,
this honourable institution
provides the needs of sundry clients;
sells hardbacks, softbacks, magazines
to urban peasants, lords, and queens.

8:06 am

Rebecca works the morning shift
behind the counter, while sporadic
parties of literati drift
between the bookshelves. Their nomadic
reconnaissance—from Crime and Mystery
through Fantasy and Science Fiction,
Biography, Romance and History,
Humour and Art—defies prediction;
they sometimes buy a favoured book,
but most just stand around and browse,
sneaking the odd repentant look
towards the staff as tact allows.
Of course, Rebecca doesn't care:
her thoughts are strictly solitaire.

8:09 am

She wonders whether she should start
her reading for the next semester.
She briefly thinks about Descartes
and pairs of purple polyester
trousers she noticed in a clearance
across the mall. She ponders karma,
thinks vaguely over her appearance,
recites a speech she learned for drama,
tries to recall this morning's dreams,
wonders what outfit she should wear
when she goes out tonight, and schemes
of how she'll be a millionaire
a few years in the future. Then,
despite herself, she thinks of Glenn.

8:12 am

She hasn't always been this way.
She never cared for anyone
substantially before the day
she met him. Her idea of fun
was different, then. She liked to party;
she'd twist and shout the whole night through.
Her appetite for drink was hearty;
she'd try most anything taboo,
and mostly had a good time trying.
Smoked marijuana now and then;
took LSD, and felt like flying,
but only once. A dozen men,
or boys, or more, had known her bed.
Their memories now fill her head.

8:15 am

As her surroundings blur and drain
of colour, and the shop distorts,
she's noticed by a colleague, Jane,
who calls, 'A dollar for your thoughts!'
Rebecca's roused from her stagnation,
and says, 'A dollar? Won't a penny
do it these days?' 'Well, that's inflation,'
Jane sighs: 'I mean, I haven't any
money to speak of anyway—
you know the wages we get paid—
hardly enough to throw away!
But if you're willing to parade
your thoughts for slightly less a fee,
then make an audience of me.'

8:18 am

Rebecca's gleaming, verdant eyes
resume their former glassy cast.
She says, 'Just thinking of the guys
I knew in my anarchic past.
Remember Jim? He rode a Harley.
Looked good in leather. Not too bright.
We'd smoke and listen to Bob Marley,
and tell each other jokes all night.
Did you meet Frank? He always thought
he'd change the world... but hasn't yet.
And Chuck? He drove a juggernaut.
He's cruising somewhere now, I bet.
Damian? David? Patrick? Paul?
I almost thought I loved them all.'

8:21 am

'What happened, then?' 'They didn't last.
A week, a month—or two at most—
and then some other suitor passed
my way. I mean, I hate to boast,
but plenty of them seemed impressed
by me. The way I looked, or danced,
or what I said, or how I dressed:
I think it had them all entranced.'
'I wish I had your problems!' Jane
exclaims. 'If your admirers flocked
to me like that, I'd not complain.
Just tell me how I might concoct,
as you have done, the magic potion
that hastens this wholesale devotion.'

8:24 am

Rebecca laughs. 'There's no trick, really.
No magic brew or voodoo prayer,
no yogi's good-luck charm. I merely
decided that a fun affair
was what I wanted. Having started,
when someone more ideal appeared,
I'd leave. No one was broken-hearted;
no heavy feelings interfered.
I cared for them much more than they
for me; they had as many girls
as I had guys. We'd always say
the undertows and unknown swirls
of love were best left unexplored:
raw passion was our smorgasbord.'

8:27 am

'But then what?' Jane is quick to hasten.
'You speak as if all this were past.
Was passion's stone hewn by a mason
so clumsy? Were you so miscast
in role that you were forced to quit?
Why else relinquish such good times?'
Rebecca smiles: 'That isn't it.
I loved it all. But pantomimes,
though fanciful and entertaining
for folk to watch, are nonetheless
to their protagonists quite draining.
It's fine to glow and effervesce,
but if that isn't how you feel,
you can't forget it isn't real.

8:30 am

'When lying in a lover's arms,
I'd wonder whether this was all
there was: a glance, the standard charms,
a night of lust. I can't recall
the faintest feeling of surprise
or any real spontaneity
when dealing with these perfect guys.
Like rituals, worshipping a deity,
the moves we made were all rehearsed:
a game to which we knew the rules.
Well-trained, well-practised, and well-versed
in all the smoothest courters' tools,
our love was more a complex dance
than anything admitting chance.'

8:33 am

'What's wrong with that?' Jane interjects.
'If you enjoyed it, I don't see
the great dilemma. Ill-effects
were minimal, correct? To me,
such dalliance with strings detached
approaches worldly paradise.
Or have your fancies somehow hatched
the notion that old-fashioned, nice,
and gallant Romeos are waiting
to sweep a girl right off her feet?
If so, your standards need updating.
Those aren't the kind of guys you meet:
they only live in verse and song.'
Rebecca smiles: 'That's where you're wrong.

8:36 am

'I felt like you do, once upon
a time. I fancied love a myth:
the purple weed of Oberon
contained no vitalising pith
as far as I could ascertain.
A fairytale of Shakespeare, Keats
and Tennyson—a false domain
of airy lies and smooth deceits—
was all I thought romance to be,
while sex was real and undisputed,
pleasure the only guarantee.
But my derision was confuted,
my scepticism silenced, when
I found what I'd thought lost. With Glenn.'

8:39 am

The sun glares like apocalypse
upon the city spread below.
The mirrored towers can't eclipse
the searing light; instead, aglow
like altar candles, they reflect
it back and forth beyond infinity.
The flaring lustre flows unchecked,
and everything in the vicinity
is washed away before the wave
that crashes through the city streets.
The heat is too intense to brave,
too ravenous to flee: it beats
upon the heads of passers-by,
who are too sunstruck to reply.

8:42 am

A gentle breeze blows round the hill
above the quarry, partly slowing
the heat that otherwise would fill
its rocky well to overflowing.
The wandering and welcome wind
ripples between the sulking leaves
of olives trees and onion-skinned
strata of time-scarred cliff. It weaves
its way between the piles of rocks,
the cataracts of scree that litter
the quarry floor, the fallen blocks
of stone. The sunlight sets aglitter
the crystal quartz that lies around;
the heat is silent and profound.

8:45 am

The quarry wall is scarred and scored
by years of miners' occupation.
Its wounds are cavernous and broad,
and further marked with fine striation.
The elements have taken toll,
hard water carving graceful grooves
descending to the rough-hewn bowl
of excavation. Wind improves
and polishes with slow erosion
the surface of the sandstone, grizzled
and chafed with gelignite explosion.
But one such scratch is neatly chiselled,
a message, in the rocky wall—
'Glenn loves Rebecca'. That is all.

8:48 am

The quarry was at first revealed
by Glenn. Located down the street
from Becca's house, behind a shield
of vegetation, so complete
was its seclusion that she'd never
stumbled across it, all the years
she'd lived beside it. Glenn, however,
with resource like a pioneer's,
unearthed it, claiming it as theirs.
A special place in both their hearts
and minds, where common, worldly cares
were soon dispelled behind ramparts
of rock and veils of trees—above
all this, it is a place of love.

8:51 am

Glenn, in a towel, wanders through
the open-plan rooms of his house.
He doesn't have a lot to do
these lazy summer mornings. Strauss
plays clamorously through the halls
at fullest volume, shaking floors
with extra bass. Glenn's clothing sprawls,
discarded, on the ground. The doors
are opened wide to catch the breeze
the weather forecast promised, now
long overdue. Glenn's Siamese,
Hermia, gives a faint miaow
of disapproval at the weather;
Glenn joins her, and they howl together.

8:54 am

Glenn's growing conscious of the fact
that he should start the tardy task
of cleaning. Piles of dishes, stacked
into a grim and wobbling masque
of treachery adorn the sink;
the carpet boasts unlikely stains
in complementary green and pink.
The lounge recalls a hurricane's
destruction, and the laundry bulges
with untold mounds of unwashed clothes.
This wholesale disarray divulges
Glenn's hidden flaw: he clearly loathes
housekeeping chores of any kind—
catastrophe he doesn't mind.

8:57 am

In fact, if he were left alone
indefinitely, he would never
confront the random chaos thrown
about the house. The dread endeavour
he faces now is a result
not of his own accord, but rather,
by the decree of the adult
to whom he answers first. His father,
away on business for the past
six weeks, is due back home tomorrow.
So Glenn must clean and tidy fast:
thus is the author of his sorrow.
He shuts his eyes, loath to address
impenetrable wealths of mess.

9:00 am

But in his mind, his labours change
into a Herculean quest
to chivalrously rearrange
the minions of disorder. Dressed
in tracksuit, substituting armour,
he contemplates his battle plan,
unfolding in his mind a drama
in honour of gods Spic and Span.
He casts himself, a noble knight,
into the hard-fought leading role,
charged to apply his cunning, might,
and skill in order to control
the dread disease that roams, unchecked,
throughout the land he must protect.

9:03 am

So, while disorder seems to reign,
its upper hand will soon be lost.
As Glenn goes on to sweat and strain
against his foe, his crimson-crossed
and shining armour will defend
against the fast-declining hordes
of mayhem, bringing to an end
their foul dominion. Glenn marauds
in gleeful triumph, washing plates
and clothes, arranging chairs and tables,
sailing away from dire straits
with skill approaching that of fables.
Victoriously he admires
his work; exhausted, he retires.

9:06 am

The phone calls out. 'Hello? Oh, hi!
How goes it, babe? That's good. I'm fine,
but hot—damn hot! I don't know why—
it's far too warm for just-past-nine.
The summer solstice? Hey, you're right!
Though why the longest day should mean
the hottest too, I don't know. Quite.
Today? At lunch? Good plan. Between
twelve and half-past? For certain. Hey,
is something wrong? Oh, nothing—you
just normally don't sound this way.
You're sure? All right. Yes, that's quite true.
You really feel okay? Right. Yeah.
Around midday—yep, I'll be there.'

9:09 am

'And what was that about?' Jane asks.
'Don't tell me "nothing", Becca dear.
I know that cool expression masks
a hint of—what? Discomfort? Fear?
If you intend to use the phone
on working time, I think it's fair
that you should make your problems known
to your most trusted colleague.' 'Yeah,'
Rebecca grins. 'I'll go find Brett.'
Jane looks distraught; Bec reassures:
'I'm joking, Jane! I've never met
such curiosity as yours!
But if you won't be happy till
I've told you, then I guess I will.

9:12 am

'It's really nothing—no, don't start.
I'm only having lunch with Glenn.
It's just—I have to break his heart
before it's over. All the men
I've broken up with, this will be
by far the hardest: I can't stand
to hurt him, but I just can't see
what else there is to do. I've planned
a dozen ways to say it: none
can painlessly convey the news.
I mean, how do you tell someone
you want to quit? To disabuse
their dreams, their clinging hopes... but, hey.
I have to. There's no other way.'

9:15 am

The mall outside Rebecca's shop
is humming with the ceaseless bustle
of people milling round to swap
cash for commodities, to hustle
the cheapest prices. Clothes that fashion
approves this season are paraded
before the marketplace's passion:
punters are easily persuaded
to sacrifice their wealth for style.
Through windows consummately dressed,
each mannequin, with painted smile,
proclaims its garb to be the best
available, while this conceit
is reinforced out in the street.

9:18 am

Among the throng of clothing stores—
fit to outfit the vainest emperor
with new ensembles fine as gauze
and colourful as richest tempera—
lie new enticements for consumers:
from hi-fi traders, gushing sound,
to newsstands, auctioning the rumours
of unconsenting authors; wound
between these stores are smaller stalls,
appearing magically at dawn
to sell their flowers to the mall's
frequenters. Old and weatherworn
constructions stand beside the new,
their aspect pleasantly askew.

9:21 am

Kristin is hauntingly reminded
of home as she meanders down
the busy mall. A moment blinded
by memory, the ochre-brown
pavestones beneath her pausing feet
seem to belong, some otherwhere,
to Copenhagen's shopping street,
the Strøget, longest thoroughfare
kept for pedestrians in all
the world, where walkers shop for furs
and scarves, not T-shirts. Though this mall
is but a parody of hers,
a common atmosphere remains
to collocate these foreign lanes.

9:24 am

She shakes off her nostalgic thoughts
and takes a look around. She's wearing
her hiking boots, her high-cut shorts
and singlet similarly daring.
The incongruity between
Kris and the local girls is subtle,
but undeniable. She's seen
the unappealable rebuttal
of any foreigner's attempt
to travel at all incognito,
and doesn't think herself exempt
from the enactment of this veto:
without a hope of emulation,
she revels in her deviation.

9:27 am

Her clothes support no kangaroo
impressions; she does not wear thongs.
Fosters is not her favoured brew,
nor does she hazard outback songs.
No stockman's hat attached with corks
adorns her head; she doesn't drawl
'g'day' or 'cobber' when she talks,
dismisses the Australian crawl
and doesn't waltz, Matilda. While
this might seem obvious to some,
it contradicts the studied style
of many travellers who come
prospecting in this land Down Under,
and tear their dignity asunder.

9:30 am

Kris notices the sly attention
bestowed on her by passers-by,
who stare with slight incomprehension
and seldom look her in the eye,
as if they can't quite understand
why anyone should want to travel
to such an ordinary land
as theirs. No secret to unravel
exists upon their doorsteps, surely:
they take their trivia for granted
and can't imagine that their poorly
and paltry lives ever enchanted
a visitor with sights to see.
Kristin, of course, would disagree.

9:33 am

A stranger in this foreign place,
Kris revels in the little things
few of its residents embrace.
Each unexpected corner brings
new marvels that impress her mind
as if it were a thirsty sponge,
incorrigibly unrefined,
naively predisposed to plunge
headlong through any new domain,
and positively parasitic
in its unstoppable campaign
of greedy learning, analytic
evaluation, record-taking:
no wonder Kristin's head is aching.

9:36 am

The rush of concrete information
impressing onto Kristin's senses—
approaching total penetration
and overwhelming her defences—
compels her to remain a while
and simply try to take it in.
Her wonder almost infantile,
she tries to comprehend the din
of noise and image, sight and smell,
flicker of colour, snatch of speech
and blur of movement that all gel
into a chaos out of reach
of reasoning or recognition:
a mystifying apparition.

9:39 am

She sees, but doesn't understand,
a hundred neatly printed signs,
the headstones of a foreign land—
their careful curves and painted lines
resist translation into words
and keep their secret meanings, though
she's fluent in their language. Herds
of monstrous people come and go,
yet never seem to move. A child
upends its ice-cream cone; vanilla
goes hurtling to the ground. A wild
Saint Nicholas grins like a killer
of children, high above the mall;
no reason lives within this thrall.

9:42 am

But as Kris starts to gain a handle
on her surroundings, they become
benevolent. The raging Vandal
thundering to his battle-drum
is suddenly a harmless street
musician; the insane applause
and bedlam strains of stamping feet
no longer deafen. Santa Claus,
so recently a psychopath,
is now a helium balloon,
bobbing above the aftermath
of her imagination. Soon,
a scene that would make Dante proud
resolves into a normal crowd.

9:45 am

The masses rushing blindly past
at once become distinct; no longer
mere atoms caught within a vast
morass, they now seem clearer, stronger.
They walk, and talk, and think, and feel;
each has a home, a love, a life;
their lively faces each conceal
decades of reminiscence, rife
with pleasure, passion, heartache, pain—
a story few will ever read,
a narrative to entertain
no audience, but to proceed
regardless, growing day by day:
an unseen, tragicomic play.

9:48 am

A thousand storylines compete
for space in her imagination,
no twist too subtle to defeat
her practised skills of observation.
She notices two lovers, strolling
with hands thrust in each other's pockets;
a spruiker, busily cajoling;
a customer demanding dockets.
Two children chase in hot pursuit
between the slowly shifting crowds.
A busker plays a soothing flute
whose lilting melody enshrouds
the palpitating thoroughfare,
and calms it with a graceful air.

9:51 am

The flautist tarries unaware
of Kristin's curious attention.
He prances, sleek and debonair,
immune to any intervention.
His crumpled, though genteel, attire—
tuxedo, top hat, tie and tails
(his own, what's more, and not for hire)—
belies the dirty fingernails,
the shoeless feet and unwashed hair
that give away the social class
of Rocky, homeless millionaire,
who tries despairingly to pass
as one of high nobility,
despite his urban pedigree.

9:54 am

As Arthur sidles up beside
the ragged rich man, Rocky scowls
with challenged and indignant pride.
'Don't bother me at work!' he growls:
'You vagrant! Bum of little fame!'
'Come off your high horse, Rockefeller,'
says Arthur: 'And renounce this game.
Admit you're just a pavement-dweller
and take your place with Ed and me.'
'This is my place!' his friend insists:
'The door was bolted, but the key
was always here between my fists—
and now I claim my true repute!'
He holds aloft his battered flute.

9:57 am

Rock notices Art's artless stare,
and cries, 'Come on, Art! Don't you get it?
My first Carnegie première
will be on this flute, you can bet it!'
'Now, let me get this straight,' Art frowns.
'You plan to play your magic pipe
and bid farewell to cabbagetowns
for good? I've never heard such tripe.
You think you'll hasten the dismissal
of all your troubles—like the rats
of Hamlin—with a penny whistle?
And this is how your vain, ersatz
nobility is to be earned?
I think your senses have adjourned.'

10:00 am

'Think what you like,' Rock says, dogmatic.
'But class can always recognise
its own. When the aristocratic
discover me, they'll realise
that I am one of them, and offer
the social standing that I've lost.
So mock me now, O lowly scoffer;
I offer you no quick riposte.
But soon your face's other side
will bear your grin, and soon your chance
to laugh will end, and all your snide
remarks will bear no *vraisemblance*.
But as my plan demands I play
my flute, I wish you'd go away.'

10:03 am

'All right. No need to tell me twice,'
Art stiffens, trying to conceal
his irritation. 'My advice
is formulated to appeal
to those who live on planet earth,
and you are not among their number,
it seems to me. It isn't worth
continuing to disencumber
you of your myths, so I'll be going.'
With this, Art turns and walks toward
a bin, replete and overflowing,
where Ed seeks to increase his hoard.
The pair prepare to wander on;
a second later, they are gone.

10:06 am

As Rock resumes his minuet,
making the flute dance in his hands,
innocent of the etiquette
that high society demands,
a pale and red-haired woman stops
and searches him with jade-green eyes.
She takes a camera out, and drops
to one knee, hoping to devise
the perfect shot. 'You don't mind, do you?'
she asks. Rock says, 'No, not at all!
Don't let my artistry subdue you;
I knew the talent scouts would call.
Now, where's my limousine? And where—'
he starts, but she's no longer there.

10:09 am

As Zoe flees the strangely-dressed
and crazy-talking shoeless man,
she contemplates again her quest,
and re-evaluates her plan.
In desperation now, she's snapped
a photo of most anything
that takes her interest, whether apt
for publishing or not. 'The sting
of my enthusiasm's dull,'
she thinks. 'I've lost the cutting edge.
These images impinge my skull,
but I've not energy to dredge
value or meaning from their ranks:
this job affords me little thanks.'

10:12 am

She leaves the mall and walks toward
the tree-lined terrace, set a block
away, where she hopes to applaud
the city's local culture stock.
Behind a fountain, past a grove
of palm trees and a well-kept lawn,
the state museum holds a trove
of relics, time-abused and worn,
a hoard of modern artifacts,
preserved menageries of creatures.
The promise of such things attracts
her expectation of new features
to kick-start her enthusiasm
and kindle her iconoclasm.

10:15 am

The skeletons of dinosaurs
receive her as she wanders through
a pair of automatic doors.
The sole remaining residue
of earth's usurped and ancient lords,
the incomplete and brittle bones
now seem malingerers and frauds,
pretenders squatting on the thrones
of kings long dead, suggesting no
reflection of their cruel glory,
and shouting no *bravissimo*
for any prehistoric story.
To look on fossil, bone and dust is
to do their memory no justice.

10:18 am

A floor above, a very ark
of animals lie trapped behind
protective plates of perspex, stark
against blank backgrounds, undersigned
with unintelligible names
in Latin, and impaled with pins.
Each vacant, vapid eye proclaims
a faint surprise, and lifeless grins
play on the lips of those deceased.
To some, this carnage represents
the worship of the living beast:
a celebration of intense
vitality, and life, and breath.
But Zoe sees here only death.

10:21 am

For how can corpses reproduce
the glory of a beast in nature?
Its freedom, joyful and profuse—
its disregard for legislature
complete—its grace and skill innate?
Such animals are not the kin
of the cadavers that prostrate
themselves unwillingly within
transparent coffins, rudely stuffed
and pickled in formaldehyde.
The flame of life, so brashly snuffed
in this methodic multicide,
still lingers, like a dead king's ghost,
but can't reanimate its host.

10:24 am

These thoughts come as no small surprise
to Zoe, who has not before
seen through such grim and bloodshot eyes.
That she has now come to deplore
these poor museum pieces proves
that she has lately lost her touch.
Disheartened, she gets up and moves
away from the exhibit. Such
a modestly macabre scene,
at once prosaic and depraved,
provides no mental gasoline
of inspiration: if she raved
about it, serious and solemn,
The New York Times would drop her column.

10:27 am

A wall adorned with hieroglyphic
designs precedes a new collection.
Leaving behind the last horrific
displays, she takes a new direction
toward the Nile's silted delta,
observing relics long preserved
beneath the time-resistant shelter
of pyramids. A touch unnerved
by such antiquity, she sees a
great majesty among these forms,
these still inhabitants of Giza
who've safely weathered all the storms
of wind and sand and time's harsh blast:
a fading echo of the past.

10:30 am

A cast of the Rosetta stone
copies the long-awaited key
to reading of this time unknown,
this ciphered book of history.
Papyrus scrolls unfold to tell
the secrets of an ancient race;
ornate sarcophagi farewell
their tenants to an unknown place.
Embraced in bandages and tar,
once-regal cats and noble hawks
accompany their lords to Ra.
No relic in this chamber talks,
but stories ring between these walls
with all the distant past recalls.

10:33 am

The only trouble with this scene
is that she's seen it all before.
Throughout her odyssey she's been
from Alexandria's far shore
to Cairo, cruising on the Nile
past the Great Pyramid, the Sphinx
and all their ancient comrades. While
evading Tutankhamen's jinx
in Egypt and worldwide museums,
she read the genuine Rosetta,
stood inside countless mausoleums
and saw displays of old far better
than any this poor chamber holds
within its spare, redundant folds.

10:36 am

So, while she cannot help but stand
enraptured by the sheer antiquity,
its news is somewhat second-hand—
and perpetrating the iniquity
of reproducing what she wrote
before, of course, is inconceivable:
the once-established anecdote
is ever after irretrievable,
never to be re-used. Unique
phenomena are all she sees
as worth her while, so she must seek
her story elsewhere. Zoe flees
the exhibition in despair,
quite weary of the whole affair.

10:39 am

As customary, inspiration
has little trouble finding Glenn.
He sits, eyes closed in concentration,
before his drawing board. His pen
is poised above a stack of papers
of different textures; now it darts
and flourishes, and now it capers:
his eyes leap open, and he starts
defining—cautiously at first—
an outline on the page. Broad strokes
take over as a deeper burst
of creativity provokes
a sense of confidence: his style
is now dynamic, volatile.

10:42 am

And now it's over. With a sketch
of utmost brevity, he's able
to reach into his mind and fetch
a passing vision. On a table
lie half a dozen recent snatches
and fragments from his mental store.
Along the walls hang older batches
to which he has devoted more
effort and artistry; these drafts
are filled in watercolour, ink
or airbrush: of Glenn's growing crafts,
these pictures show a special link
among the images that rush
between his fancy and his brush.

10:45 am

Glenn's studio is thus bedecked
with pictures, hanging wall to wall,
combining smoothly to project
an epic story through the sprawl
of papers in a crude mosaic
that spreads across the room. Its major
motif is chivalrous, archaic;
its subject is a brave teenager
with sandy hair and grey-blue eyes;
its setting ranges through fantastic
formations under blood-red skies
through which our bold, enthusiastic
hero pursues his secret quest:
a knight in exile, dispossessed.

10:48 am

The epic's genesis portrays
the warrior among his friends.
Through halcyon and lazy days,
their peaceful happiness extends
through panels painted gentle green
among the village's great trees
and undergrowth. As comrades lean
against each other, grouped in threes
and fours and quaffing joyful ale,
a sense of prologue is profound:
the promise of a mighty tale
imbues the air, and wafts around
the sturdy oaks and slender pines
that Glenn's fine artistry defines.

10:51 am

A panel later, and our knight
is guest of honour at a feast.
A spread of edible delight
supplies the greatest and the least
together, weighing down the tables
around a blazing bonfire—which
with welcome heat and light enables
the mood to keep its perfect pitch
long through the darkest night. With laughter
our hero leads his kin and friends
in hearty conversation; after
the banquet—when the party ends—
is time best left unthought, ignored:
the present is its own reward.

10:54 am

But time must march steadfastly on,
not always to the benefit
of those its forces fall upon.
Next day, the firmament is split
by bolts of lightning, and the sun
eclipsed by banks of angry cloud,
creating night of day. No one
goes anywhere, or talks aloud,
but, quivering in superstition,
they huddle in their huts, awaiting
the fury's gradual attrition.
The storm shows no sign of abating,
but rages solid through the morning,
as if it were foreboding, warning.

10:57 am

Appearing through the clouds, a light
shines like the golden sun; it weaves
towards the earth and sparkles bright
against the gravestone grey. As thieves
steal furtively, so too it fences
around the village in its caution,
anonymous until it senses
its opportunity. Its torsion
gives way to a direct approach;
its character grows plain at last:
it spreads its scaly wings to broach
the wind—then, with a fiendish blast
the dragon breathes a ball of fire
and swoops on the defenceless shire.

11:00 am

It lands within the village square.
Folding its wings, it slowly walks
towards our hero's house. The air
is sulphurous and poisoned; stalks
of grass and flowers singe beneath
the monster's fourfold feet. It roars
indifferently, displaying teeth
like yellow knives, crawls through the doors
and finds itself inside the hut;
it takes the hero's mother's hand
between its jaws, and clamps them shut.
Nobody moves: transfixed, they stand
as, lazily, it turns around
and drags her, wailing, to the ground.

11:03 am

Only our hero undertakes
to free his mother from its grasp;
he is the only one who breaks
free of the trembling, fearful clasp
that leaves the rest immobile still.
He sets upon the beast bare-handed—
as if he had the strength to kill
the brute—to no effect. Left stranded,
hopelessly earthbound as the fiend
lifts skyward, he can only curse
its disappearing shape. Demeaned
and impotent, he's left to nurse
his pain and rage and injured pride
alone: a hurt that won't subside.

11:06 am

His friends and family emerge
and know his efforts are in vain.
Silent and wordless, they converge
on him and try to ease his pain.
They shrug, console, and reassure
that there was nothing he could do
to save his mother's life. Demure,
apologetic, they know too
that he resents their lack of trying.
Unable ever to forgive
their witnessing his mother's dying—
not helping, going on to live
when she is gone—he shrugs away
their hypocritical display.

11:09 am

The village setting disappears
as he begins his solo trek.
The quest for which he volunteers
has no clear ending, but the wreck
that he perceives his home to be
can offer him no further cheer:
he has no option but to flee.
From time to time his friends draw near
to keep him company: he lets
them walk with him, but doesn't speak
to anyone. Soon he forgets
how long he's travelled: days? A week?
A month, or more? He doesn't care,
lost in the vastness of despair.

11:12 am

Only his father now remains
beside him as he trudges on,
but even the old man maintains
a fluctuating presence: gone
for weeks on end, he reappears
dependably, but just as sure
is his next leaving. 'Son, careers
don't stop for grief,' he says: 'The cure
for sorrow is to live your life
more fully. I know how you feel:
you've lost a mother; I, a wife.
Don't be undone by this ordeal:
be glad to live another day.
She would have wanted it that way.'

11:15 am

The young man looks upon the other
with unconcealed contempt and scorn.
To think no more about his mother—
forget that she was ever born—
is worse than treason or sedition.
The old man is henceforth confined
to background; like an apparition
he hovers, faint and ill-defined,
unheeded by the younger man
as, banishing all comradeship,
estranged from village, home and clan,
imprisoned by the frozen grip
of solitude, hard, cold as stone,
our hero wanders on—alone.

11:18 am

Alone he walks through forests, rich
and speckled different shades of green,
where birds assume a muffled pitch
as he traverses velveteen
carpets of moss from tree to tree.
Alone he climbs tall mountains, rough
and rugged under clouds that flee
their jagged reaches; over bluff
and broad escarpment, through crevasse
and canyon, under skies on fire
with random, richly-coloured gas
like halting Vulcan's smithy pyre—
our hero travels ever on,
an obstinate automaton.

11:21 am

Now even strangers cease to pass
his way; insensate to this lack,
he walks through scenery grown sparse:
the earth beneath his feet turns black
beneath the gnarled and hunchbacked trees
that crouch like skeletons around
the rocks, misshapen with disease,
that mark the scorched and wasted ground.
No features pierce the far horizon;
the land is uniformly flat.
Our hero trudges, with his eyes on
the barren dirt before him; fat
thunderheads dim this place passed over
by Baal, abandoned by Jehovah.

11:24 am

The warrior continues through
a dozen panels, all alike:
all trace of colour, shade or hue
is banished; the tyrannic reich
of black and dismal watercolour
now rules these claustrophobic frames,
growing forever darker, duller.
The muddy wilderness proclaims
the mood of hero and of muse,
for Glenn is echoed in his work,
the wanderer's oppressive blues
afflicting both. Glenn gives a smirk
as he reviews this section now:
it seems less pertinent, somehow.

11:27 am

For as our hero stumbles, weary,
across the endless deathscape, he
looks up at last across the dreary
arc of horizon—he can see
no variation in its curve,
save one far, indistinct protrusion
that seems to deviate and swerve
along a path of vague confusion.
And as the speck grows closer, bigger,
he squints in order to make out
what seems to be a human figure;
and suddenly an ancient drought
is broken, and it rains anew
as fellow life pulls into view.

11:30 am

The figure seems to notice him,
and redirects its path toward
our wanderer—whose face is grim
but hopeful, hand upon his sword
from habit more than ill intent.
He notes the figure's foreign style
of dress and arms as its ascent
continues steadily. Exile
no longer in our hero's mind,
he shuns companionship no more.
Approaching, he's surprised to find
the warrior he stands before
is female: a crusading queen
with jet-black hair and eyes of green.

11:33 am

She reaches, now, and takes his hand,
forcing his eyes and head to follow
upwards. He finds that he can stand
aloft, where he could only wallow
in misery and mud. She leads
him on like this until his strength
returns, and his despair recedes
before a new-found hope. At length
the scenery becomes more mellow;
grass sprouts between the blackened rocks;
the sun flares in triumphant yellow
behind the thinning clouds. The pox
that once diseased the land is cured;
our hero's happiness, assured.

11:36 am

It isn't hard to recognise
that Glenn's most secret and internal
philosophies make their disguise
within this story. It's his journal:
though writing's not his strongest suit,
he's always felt compelled to capture
the incidents that constitute
his life—that sadden and enrapture
and terrify in equal parts.
His favoured medium is drawing,
and so he sublimates his heart's
reflections in his pictures, pouring
thoughts and events into each frame—
autobiography's his aim.

11:39 am

As Glenn works on, Hermia leaps
onto his drawing table, sending
his papers to the floor in heaps,
and somewhat prematurely ending
his flurry of inspired scrawling.
She butts her head against his nose
and turns before genteelly sprawling
across his current work. Repose
this regal can't be interfered with:
Glenn rises, glances at the clock,
announces, 'Shit!' and jumps, still smeared with
inkstain and spatter, smudge and splotch.
'Rebecca! Bye, cat! I'll be late!
I gotta go! Can't let her wait!'

11:42 am

The sun creeps slowly towards noon,
as shadows gather close around
their casters, shrinking tightly, soon
to vanish from the baking ground.
Swinging directly overhead,
the sun's control becomes complete
as those beneath its power shed
their clothes to overcome the heat,
perspire and pant without relief,
search fruitlessly for scraps of shade,
however minimal or brief,
to shelter from the centigrade
that beats with no respite and no
escape: there's nowhere else to go.

11:45 am

As Kristin walks, she wonders whether
she could have picked less fitting clothes:
her singlet sticks to her; the leather
wrapping her hiking boots betroths
her feet to swelling, blains and blisters;
across her face and neck and arms
a sheen of perspiration glisters;
a shroud of stifling heat embalms
her body as a whole. It rarely
gets warm as this in Denmark; during
her travels she's becoming fairly
accustomed to extremes, but curing
her northern heritage takes time;
and mercury won't halt its climb.

11:48 am

She's met by an antarctic blast
of air exhaled into the street
as she limps resolutely past
a bookshop's open doors. The heat
outside obliges her to enter
this temporary, frigid haven:
she silently thanks the inventor
of air-conditioning, whose graven
image adorns each hallowed corner,
grinding and murmuring to cool
the shop—which would become a sauna
without this necessary tool.
Outside, the weather's hot and vile,
so Kris decides to stay a while.

11:51 am

She cruises aisle by well-stocked aisle,
past brick-sized million-selling novels,
through racks of works more juvenile,
arranged in literary hovels
encamped like refugees around
the floor. From hard to paperback,
a sad and long-forsaken mound
of old remainders forms a stack
that tries hard to retain its pride
despite the signs that read 'Marked down!',
'Pay what you like!', and 'More inside!'
Books of more coveted renown
grace this week's prized best-seller list,
a lure few buyers can resist.

11:54 am

A piece of Northern Europe finds
itself upon these southern shelves:
today it touchingly reminds
Kris of her childhood as she delves
into that finest realm of fiction—
the world of Jansson's Moomintroll,
the pudgy Finn with an addiction
to bold adventure. From his pole
the Hemulen joins Snufkin, Sniff,
the Snork and Maiden, and the rest,
in Kristin's reminiscence. If
the peaceful Moomins are impressed
by their new home, it's hard to tell:
they seem to have adapted well.

11:57 am

As Kristin's winding path addresses
another separated section,
her sentimental mood regresses
still further, through a proud collection
of timeless works by Dr Seuss.
Enchanted with *Green Eggs and Ham*
and *Thidwick, the Big-Hearted Moose,*
with repetition, tetragram,
cats in their hats, and coloured fish,
advice to never 'Hop on Pop',
the Once-ler's ecologic wish
(the fable of a new Aesop)—
Kristin is pleased to pass the time
with such outstanding works of rhyme.

12:00 pm

With true delight she finds the most
impressive rhyming book to date,
and thumbs it through, at once engrossed:
it's Vikram Seth's *The Golden Gate.*
Responsible for the revival
of history's most proud tradition
of epic poems, its arrival
fulfils its chivalrous ambition
to reinstate the sonnet form
unto its former glory, saving
tetrameter, too, from the storm
of careless history, and paving
the way for others on the list
(at least one is known to exist).

12:03 pm

She wanders onward, slyly browsing
through mammoth works by Stephen King,
while trying to avoid arousing
any suspicion that might bring
the staff to notice she's not buying,
but reading free of charge. Remaining
hidden behind the never-dying
volumes of *Life in Hell* (Matt Groening),
she sneaks a look at the assistant
behind the counter to ensure
that her attention tarries distant.
Alas! Her peek is premature:
she's met by the assistant's stare
and quickly turns her gaze elsewhere.

12:06 pm

Rebecca notices the glance
offered discreetly from the Humour
collection. Though she can't advance
a reason why this strange consumer
should grant her such an enigmatic
evaluation, in that second
she finds the contact quite dramatic,
and soon a multitude of fecund
imaginings flow from that glimpse,
the kind she's never seen before—
as mischievous as any imp's,
yet heavy with a hidden store
of meaning that she can't discern,
and probably will never learn.

12:09 pm

'Is that the time?' she says to Jane:
'My shift has never gone so fast.
Maybe I'll stay—what would I gain
by leaving now? I can't be arsed.'
Jane smiles supportively: 'You may
as well just get the whole thing over
and done with. Every hour—or day—
you leave it, like a supernova
it just gets that much more intense,
harder to deal with. You'll be fine,
just do it. You know it makes sense.'
Bec smiles back: 'How could I decline
such sound and sensible advice—
direct, well-meaning, and concise?'

12:12 pm

She turns and leaves the bookshop, wincing
as she steps out into the heat
of unconditioned air. Convincing
herself that there is no retreat,
she executes successive tacks
to dodge the traffic and arrive
at her objective: Kerouac's
Café, a trendy downtown dive.
It's named for its location, nearly
but not quite *On the Road*—the seating
(tables, umbrellas, chairs) is clearly
safe on the pavement, but if cheating
a few feet brings more clientele,
it's near enough, and just as well.

12:15 pm

She sits beneath a sun umbrella,
twisting it lazily, distracted.
Rotating like a slow propeller,
it casts dim shadows of refracted
sunlight in murky orange-red
flicking across the sidewalk. Tables
on either side of hers are spread
with glasses, food and wine, a Babel's
parade of gesture, conversation
and variably spoken tones
of laughter, passion, indignation:
as this familiar static drones
in constant, cheery background noise,
she tries to reassert her poise.

12:18 pm

A passing waiter smoothly glides
across the walk to where she sits
and takes her order. She decides
to savour a Chinotto; it's
too hot for latte, cappuccino,
even espresso. Then she calls:
'No, hang on, waiter—make it vino!
We're headed for some tricky squalls;
I'd rather have a drink inside me.'
He curtly nods and disappears;
Bec wonders, 'Drink! Will that provide me
a barricade against my tears?
Martini, maybe—whiskey fizz,
or absinthe—oh, God! There he is!'

12:21 pm

Glenn jogs along the street toward
the café. Late, he has no time
to dodge the never-ending horde
of shoppers, litter, dirt and grime
that clog the narrow sidewalks: taking
to bitumen, he pounds the road
along its centre, madly making
his way between the stop-light-slowed
columns of traffic, deftly tracing
his way along the painted line
as if it were a tightrope. Racing
to safety as the once-benign
machines resume their heated chase,
he slows, and walks with utmost grace.

12:24 pm

Thus sauntering, he finds Rebecca
inspecting absently—detached—
the red-white geometric chequer
of plastic tablecloth, long scratched
by hungry and impatient diners.
He thinks she hasn't seen him, stalks
around a party of designers
engaged in champagne-livened talks,
and pounces straight into his chair,
intending ambush. She looks up:
'Hi, Glenn. I didn't see you there.
Sit down—oh, yeah, you are. A cup
of coffee? Maybe something stronger?
I couldn't hold out any longer.'

12:27 pm

'Why not?' says Glenn, a little nervous:
she doesn't often drink at lunch—
is something wrong? 'I hope they'll serve us
before too long.' He has a hunch,
ignores it. 'Sorry I'm so late—
am I forgiven?' 'I suppose,'
Rebecca answers: 'Maybe fate
detained you... destiny? Who knows?'
Glenn laughs, and leans across to kiss
her quickly on the lips. She shrinks,
recoiling slightly. 'What's all this?
Didn't I brush my teeth?' Glenn thinks.
She grins to reassure, but he's
already conscious of unease.

12:30 pm

He starts to talk, but Bec is quicker:
'So, how are you today? What's new?'
Her warmth extinguishes his flicker
of doubt; informal interview
takes over. 'Good, not much; I cleaned
the house this morning—Dad gets back
tomorrow, did you know?—sardined
my stuff in drawers and cupboards. Slack,
I know, I really should have folded
my clothes and organised them properly.
I'm sure my mother would have scolded,
but she had absolute monopoly
on tidiness, and now she's gone,
we men are left to jumble on.'

12:33 pm

'What would you do without us girls?'
Bec quips, unmeaningly ironic.
'I hope I won't find out.' Glenn hurls
a smile that cuts her with demonic
brutality, despite intention;
again she flinches. Glenn continues,
unmindful of her apprehension,
which clenches teeth and tightens sinews
in order to avoid betraying
her inner turmoil. Concentrating
so hard, she's not sure what he's saying
(Hermia? Drawing?)—fascinating
as Glenn's forenoon may well have been,
she's in a wholly other scene.

12:36 pm

But both their worlds are interjected
by the arrival of a waiter,
who wants to know if they've selected,
or if he'd better come back later.
They study hastily but slowly:
'The vermicelli? Tortellini?
A slice of pizza? Ravioli?'
'Perhaps spaghetti... fettuccine?'
'Some garlic bread, and cannelloni,'
Glenn finally elects. Bec favours
a salad with some macaroni;
gelati for dessert: 'What flavours?
Strawberry? Mango? Apricot?
I can't decide—give me the lot!'

12:39 pm

Rebecca drains her Sangiovese
and signals for another. 'Yikes!'
Glenn teases, smiling: 'Don't go crazy!'
'Why can't a girl drink what she likes?'
'She can—of course,' he says, retreating.
An awkward silence fills the space
between them, while the people eating
around them murmur, deep in bass
and shrill in treble, glasses clinking,
cutlery scraping, laughter rising—
the silence of Rebecca thinking
is louder than all these, surprising
her consort, who had not expected
to be so voicelessly neglected.

12:42 pm

It's now Glenn's turn to interrupt,
just as she starts to speak. A fear
has reached inside him, fingers cupped
around his heart: he's loath to hear
whatever she's about to say.
With growing panic he recalls
the distant and distracted way
she spoke this morning; now he stalls
in order to avoid the truth
he'd earlier demanded—seeking
postponement's short-surviving ruth,
he saves himself, for now, by speaking:
'But how are you? How was the shop
this morning? Tell me all! Don't stop!'

12:45 pm

Rebecca pauses, changing tack.
She's not ungrateful for the chance
to detour past the cul-de-sac
her unavoidable advance
is bound for; for a while, at least,
she'll let her reason be persuaded
that happiness has not yet ceased,
her reverie as yet unfaded.
She moulds her face into a smile
and presses on: 'The shop? Not bad!
A little quiet for a while,
but that was all right; I was glad
to have the chance to do some reading:
just the refreshment I've been needing.

12:48 pm

'I sold some books. The time went by.
I had a rambling conversation
with Jane—oh, yeah! There was this guy
who almost caused an altercation:
he handed me a new release
and said, "Have many people bought it?
I heard it was a masterpiece."
I told him, "No, in fact I thought it
was boring, tedious and flat."
He winced and said, "Well, that'll show me."
I said, "What do you mean by that?"
He looked hurt, and said: "Don't you know me?"
And so I took a closer look—
and it was him, who wrote the book!'

12:51 pm

They laugh, spontaneously, freely:
a laugh of past times, recollection
and memory. Rebecca's steely
resolve and morbid introspection
are cast aside by this, the sound
she didn't know that she'd forgotten.
Glad thoughts and feelings now surround
her mind in webs of fine-spun cotton,
dulling and muting trepidation,
and relegating to obscurity
all hint of doubt or consternation,
replacing it with a security
she knows is false and will be lost,
coating her mental permafrost.

12:54 pm

She shakes away this truant feeling,
fighting the treacherous temptation
that sends her best intentions reeling
in search of cowardly placation.
How easy does retreat now seem!
How welcome is the thought of falling
compliantly into the dream
she once knew! She can hear it calling:
beckoning, wheedling, coaxing, luring,
increasingly insistent, loud
beyond all prospect of enduring
its contradiction with avowed
objectives such as Bec embraces—
it stalks her with undying paces.

12:57 pm

So influential is the lure
of this undignified escape
that for a moment she is sure
she can't resist it. Left agape,
unspeaking, she can't find the tongue
to represent her inner leaning,
her vocal cords too tightly strung
to utter any sound of meaning.
She swallows and collects her thoughts,
intent on conquering resistance.
a new-found courage now exhorts
her, with imperative insistence,
to speak. Her nerve, triumphant, thrives—
just as the *à la carte* arrives.

1:00 pm

Now, parmesan is sprinkled; forks
are seized with glee, and serviettes
arranged on laps. Now tomahawks
are buried, and unspoken debts
forsaken for the task at hand.
Anticipatory expressions
of glee bring faces to expand
in greedy grins, as all digressions
are necessarily postponed.
Glenn chews like one possessed, but Bec
pokes at the dish that she's disowned,
no longer hungry, loath to peck
the food that now seems bland as stover.
She looks up and says, 'Glenn—it's over.'

1:03 pm

Zoe stands still, her legs apart,
arms crossed, a hand upon her chin.
She gazes at the work of art
before her, a bemused half-grin
playing across her features. Framed
extravagantly and ornately,
this masterpiece has been proclaimed
a prime attraction of the stately
art gallery through which she wanders,
seeking to be inspired. *Still Life*
with Hedgehog and Two Anacondas
does not impress her, neither *Wife*
of Artist, Dressed as Elton John.
She shrugs, exhales, and ambles on.

1:06 pm

Some tolerable art is hung
around her, but it can't compete
with everything she's seen among
the world's great galleries, replete
with wonders—from the Spanish Prado
to New York's Guggenheim and Met
(the city-dweller's El Dorado);
the Vatican museums, set
with still the world's most famous ceiling;
the Tate, and the Musée d'Orsay;
the Iron Curtain torn, revealing
Pergamon, wondrous disarray
of Hermitage—all these are great;
comparison can devastate.

1:09 pm

'Perhaps I'm doing this all wrong,'
thinks Zoe. 'For there must be more
to culture than the endless throng
of trinkets by the groaning floor.
How may I know the secret hidden
within this town? How can I find
and chew upon this fruit forbidden—
this knowledge? All I taste is rind,
the flesh lost to my stranger's teeth.
If only those who live here would—'
She stops and freezes, as beneath
a cartoon lightbulb. 'Well, I could—
why not? In order to unmask
this place, I only need to ask!'

1:12 pm

At length, Kris finds a lunching spot
within her economic reach.
It's slower than McDonald's, not
as ritzy as a Sunset Beach
hotel, but every bit as cheap
as anywhere Kris cares to mention.
The wealth of edibles to reap
within its walls snares her attention:
with fingers long, green and organic,
the market beckons her inside;
life-saving, selfless, messianic,
its solemn pledge is to provide
a low-cost, satisfying crust—
a promise she can't help but trust.

1:15 pm

Within, a flowing cornucopia
of alimentary delight
assails her senses. The utopia
contained in countless satellite
shops, stalls and barrows makes her feel
a kid within a candy store,
amazed, unable to conceal
her wonder at the sight of more
abundant, rich and varied foods
than she's beheld in quite a while.
Dwarfed by such towered multitudes
of sustenance, she wanders, aisle
by aisle, throughout this paradise
of quality and marked-down price.

1:18 pm

She pauses by a nearby stall,
loaded with cheeses, young and vintage,
with discs of edam, large and small:
thick coins produced by dairy mintage.
Half-lost pie-charts of camembert,
blue fingers snaking gorgonzola,
havarti, wensleydale, gruyere—
from equatorial to polar,
the carpets of fine cheese that stretch
in front of Kristin's hungry eyes
would fill a Monty Python sketch.
She can't decide or compromise
between them, but she buys a slice
of gouda for a modest price.

1:21 pm

A crusty bread roll from the baker's,
and Kristin's banquet is complete.
She leaves the market for the acres
of parkland set across the street,
and makes her picnic on a bench.
She reaches for her bag, and drains
half of her water flask to quench
the morning's thirst and cool her veins.
She wonders when she ever ate
a more fulfilling meal: unable
to think of any dinner-date
or lavishly-spread banquet table
affording her more satisfaction,
she slips into well-fed inaction.

1:24 pm

Above her, swaying evergreens
form living, breathing canopies,
and paperbarks draw tactful screens.
A barely noticeable breeze
blows like a kiss; no one perceives
the ripple its faint breath provokes.
The sun comes dazzling through the leaves,
recalling Tennyson. The cloaks
of greenery diffuse and mute
the light; the searing summer glare
is softened, and an attribute
of gentle stillness casts the air
as if by magic. Shadows dapple
the ground like stained glass in a chapel.

1:27 pm

The parklands wrap the city centre,
connecting in a circling band
that anybody who would enter
the city must pass over. Planned
meticulously, and designed
at once to insulate, control
and beautify, it's rare to find
so undisturbed and (mostly) whole
a strip of nature so preserved
from metropolitan advance.
Its accolades are well-deserved:
without it, Kris would have no chance
to doze, serenely and discreet,
beside this jungle of concrete.

1:30 pm

Glenn's aspect, too, resembles sleep:
head buried in his palms, eyes pressed
tight shut as he attempts to keep
the world removed, at bay. Caressed
and shielded by this vain defence,
with only hands and hair exposed,
he tries to challenge the immense
encumbrance settling, unopposed,
against his slumping back, bent neck,
retreating, beaten shoulders. Fading
echoes of words bounce round the wreck
behind his clutching hands, parading
their hateful message through his head.
He vaguely wishes he were dead.

1:33 pm

'Explain it to me one more time—'
His breaking words come muffled, bare,
making their faint, uncertain climb
through murky depths of hands and hair.
'What did I do? Where did I fail?
How did I make a tragedy
out of our living fairytale?
It makes no sense—I just don't see—
what did I ever do to hurt you?
When did I ever let you down?
How did I manage to divert you
away from me? How did I drown
our passion's flame with soapsuds, bland
and dull? I just don't understand.'

1:36 pm

'It's not like that—' Rebecca falters.
'—It's really not like that at all.
I can't explain—look, nothing alters
the fact I care for you—I'd call
you, still, my best friend ever. But
I just can't handle life around you.
My God, I must sound like a nut...
I almost wish I'd never found you—
you should have left me well alone.
We've not a thing in common—friends,
work, uni, fun—I've never known
two people less alike! Our trends
run opposite—our paths don't cross!
Can you explain? I'm at a loss!'

1:39 pm

Red-faced, damp-eyed, with trembling lips
and hands, she stops and looks away;
her locks of jet-black hair eclipse
her face from Glenn's. Slowly, a stray
teardrop breaks free and slides toward
her jaw, traversing flushing cheeks.
She wipes it off; she can't afford
to tolerate unruly leaks—
whether salt water or emotion.
Behind her tempered gates of will,
she holds a potent, seething ocean
of fearsome feeling—which might kill
her if she let it beat her—like
a finger sealing up a dyke.

1:42 pm

Despite her pains, Glenn sees her tears—
mascara running, eyes averted.
As if for the first time, he hears
the words she's uttered. Disconcerted,
denied the doubtful consolation
of anger and resent to ease
his shock and hurt and indignation,
he now feels pain and pity. She's
so unprotected and exposed
before him that he wants to reach
across and comfort her—enclosed
in loving arms and tender speech—
to shield her from her bitter chill.
He knows he cannot, and is still.

1:45 pm

Along the street, the market teems
with languid after-lunch activity,
processing customers in streams
somewhat reduced by the declivity
that follows on the midday rush.
Behind the gaudy, bright facade—
the painted wood, clean floors and lush
displays of produce—lies the yard
where trucks grind in and out each morning,
where workers sweat transporting food,
where giant skips and bins lie yawning,
mouths gaping with a plenitude
of rotting cabbages, green meat,
and fruit too old and bruised to eat.

1:48 pm

Zen stumbles on this bulging chasm
of edibles just past their prime
with undisguised enthusiasm.
Employing nearby drums to climb
atop a waste-bin's drooling lip,
she launches at the scrap-heap towering
inside the battered garbage skip,
sniffing at long-gone cheese, devouring
sumptuous morsels of old rind.
She leaps from peak to mouldy peak,
delighted by her startling find,
unmindful of the pungent reek
that drives away the hoi polloi;
she wags her tail, and barks for joy.

1:51 pm

Abandoned on the edge of town,
a lonely, half-grown German shepherd
whose owners couldn't bear to drown
or shoot their pup, her life's been peppered
with peril. Countless night arrests,
death sentences avoided barely,
food begged or stolen, Zen suggests
a Dickens character. She's rarely
held down a job: though the police
recruited her, once, from the pound,
she wasn't fit to keep the peace,
deciding she was always bound,
instead of charging discipline,
to view the doghouse from within.

1:54 pm

Before long, she became well-known
among the city employees
who worked the pound. Sometimes a bone
or scrap of take-away Chinese
would find its way into her cell,
donated by a friendly warden
hidden among the personnel.
Her time inside began to broaden
to weeks and months; her fateful day
of execution never came,
though no one on the staff would say
why this was so: they levelled blame
among themselves, but all could see
they'd simply have to set her free.

1:57 pm

And so, parole in paw, she walked,
a fugitive to roam at large:
her weary sometime captors balked
at execution; with the charge
that violating her probation
again would find them much less lenient,
they liberated the Alsatian—
suspended sentence more convenient
than painless, heartless euthanasia,
since she'd become a friend to all.
With the expedient erasure
of records, and advice—'Don't call!
Don't come to dinner! Be a stranger!'—
they freed the urbanite bushranger.

2:00 pm

Of course, she rode the Black Maria
on many subsequent occasions,
but someone always came to free her,
providing eloquent persuasions
of innocence that any lawyer
would be delighted to deliver—
for Zen was never a destroyer
of property, much less a giver
of grief to anyone. It seemed
that in her exile she'd befriended
the city's homeless, and been deemed
their mascot, who should be defended
through thick and thin—and it's well known
that they look after all their own.

2:03 pm

Now, tiring of her gourmandising,
she carefully selects a bone
particularly appetising
and leaves her paradise, the groan
of hunger silenced and appeased.
She wanders, sniffing, up the street,
tail wagging, eyes bright, grinning, pleased
to walk among so many feet
so freely. Friendly café-owners
and city workers shout her name
in cheerful greeting; sometime donors
of food and shelter do the same.
But one of lower moral stature
appears behind: it's the dog-catcher.

2:06 pm

It isn't anyone she knows,
nor has her fame impressed him yet:
she lacks the power to propose
an amnesty. He has no net,
unlike the villains of cartoons,
but whips a chain around her throat
and pulls. Indignant pride balloons
inside her, but no antidote
to this injustice is apparent.
She's dragged humiliatingly
along the street behind this arrant
incompetent, an escapee
recaptured in an epilogue—
until a voice cries: 'That's my dog!'

2:09 pm

It's Arthur, hurrying across
the street, and Ed's not far behind.
'My friend! You've remedied my loss!
I'm overjoyed that you should find
this man's best friend.' The catcher looks
suspicious: 'This your dog? You sure?'
'I ask you—do we seem like crooks?
Of course it is. I can't endure
to be without her—quite a stir
surrounds her absence!' 'Hang on, just
a minute—where's the licence, sir?'
Art pats his pockets: 'Damn—I must
have left it in my Gucci slacks...
or maybe in my Filofax?'

2:12 pm

The warden laughs. 'A likely tale.
Just register your dog in future.
I don't think you could meet the bail
if I decided to dispute your
possession of the canine—right?'
'You're right—I left my AmEx Gold
back in the Hilton room last night.
I almost wish I hadn't sold
the Rolls Royce, now! But you don't need
to hear my troubles. Thanks for Zen.
We'll disappear with all our speed.'
'I'll leave you people to it, then.
He's a good dog. I'll let him be.'
He leaves; Art mutters, 'It's a *she.*'

2:15 pm

'You didn't know me as I was
before I met you,' Bec explains.
'For that I'm sort of glad, because
I don't think you'd have liked me—brains
were never my forté back then!
My life was carefree, easy; thought
was optional, no acumen
requested of me, and my sport
was not philosophy but fun.
But most of all, I felt secure,
for I was in control: no one
could injure me; no paramour
possessed my mind such that his leaving
brought any but the slightest grieving.

2:18 pm

'But this is something other—you
must realise that. My waking hours
and nightly dreams alike pursue
your image—nothing else! My powers
of reason are impaired; the blame
is also yours. I'm scared as hell.
And vulnerable—you could maim
me with a word—with silence! Dwell
on that a moment and you'll see
that I can't live beneath this fear
and doubt. It simply isn't me.
It's not my place to pioneer
this dangerous and dark new land—
I'm going home. Please understand.'

2:21 pm

'You think that you're the only one
who has a past? It isn't so.
Consider me, Bec. I'm the son
of nobody: I had to grow
up by myself, Dad always jetting
off somewhere else for work. It's hard
to go through all that without letting
it change you—and don't disregard
she died when I was just fourteen.
You know how many friends I've had
since then? Just one. Real friends, I mean.
The ones you trust. The ones you're glad
to share your heart with, even through
it all. Just one. And that one's you.

2:24 pm

'You talk of pain. But do you know
just what it's like—' '—I do! Of course
I know it; there's no need to go
through it again. Yes, your remorse
surpasses mine—we're talking death!
Cancer! Your mother! You're a martyr
to rival all who lost their breath
through history—*Desiderata*
was modelled after you! I can't
do anything about it, though.
Don't look to me—I won't supplant
your parents, Glenn: you have to go
and get on with your life, while I
get on with mine. That's it. Goodbye.'

2:27 pm

So, tiring of Glenn's self-absorbed
mentality, Rebecca leaves.
The painful picture she's just daubed
in front of him is true; he weaves
a tapestry of woe familiar
and thus contemptible. His life
and all its matching memorabilia—
his stories, worries, tales of strife—
can be no longer her concern.
Her time with Glenn taught her to care,
a lesson that she must unlearn
if she hopes ever to repair
the deep impression that remains
imprinted on her shell-shocked brains.

2:30 pm

Zo sees a likely candidate
for questioning. She hopes to glean
his knowledge, and so obviate
the fruitless, profitless routine
of mapping terra incognita,
and solving for herself the puzzle
this town presents. She feels a cheater,
but if this place thinks it can muzzle
a travel columnist, or plot
to hide itself from the outlander,
it's wrong. For every Gordian knot
there comes a hasty Alexander:
impatiently, she draws her sword
and slices through the tangled cord.

2:33 pm

'Why do you live here, sir?' 'Excuse me?'
'Why do you live here? What's the reason?
I have to know, so don't refuse me!'
The man thinks. 'Well, the football season
is long, the TV news is short,
on Sundays you can sit at home
all day and watch "Wide World of Sport",
the dry air doesn't rust the chrome
on cars, there isn't much pollution,
the roads meet perpendicularly...
I think that's it.' With this Confucian
philosophy, particularly
mundane as it may be, he quits—
as if that's all his time permits.

2:36 pm

She notes his tale, exasperated
at having spent her precious time
on one so unsophisticated,
and tries another: 'Madam? I'm
just wondering—' 'Oh, God! What is it?
Are you a mugger?' 'No, I'm not—'
'Well, take the money! My exquisite
pearl necklace! Earrings! Take the lot!'
'I'm sorry, you've misunderstood—'
'Then take the credit cards! Don't shoot,
for I'm unarmed!' 'I'm not a hood—
believe me, I don't want your loot!
I only wanted to complete—'
But she's gone running up the street.

2:39 pm

'I won't be beaten,' Zo resolves.
'I'll find some sensible assistance
among these folk if it involves
a lifetime of unbent persistence.'
But soon her feelings turn to rage:
'Are all these people of the phylum
non compos mentis? Does no sage
inhabit this deranged asylum?
Or maybe that's the town's unique
attraction: everyone's a fool—
psychotic, schizophrenic, freak—
and eccentricity's the rule
instead of being the exception!'
She's satisfied with this perception.

2:42 pm

But Zoe nonetheless endeavours,
with flagging confidence, to try
at least once more before she severs
all hope that the vox populi
will speak in her direction. Spotting
a youth—hair sandy, grey-blue eyes—
she goes to seek his help, allotting
to him the chance to realise
her last best hope: 'Kind sir—I'm lost!
This town is large, and I'm a stranger,
but if you live here, you'll have crossed
it many times. So don't endanger
my job, but tell me, please: is there
a special place here—anywhere?'

2:45 pm

By reflex, Glenn's imagination
conjures a rolling mental picture:
the quarry, high in elevation
and spirits, peaceful—but a stricture
addresses his distracted musing,
imposed in icy tones by reason
and rationality, refusing
to listen to the polished treason
of reverie and fond delusion.
What once brought pleasure now inspires
nothing but pain by its inclusion
in memory, and lonely mires
now seep across its wondrous face.
He says, 'No. I've no special place.'

2:48 pm

Of course, the quarry still exists.
Like some elusive Brigadoon,
this place of love, of midnight trysts
and magic times, is quite immune
to Glenn's denial. Though its function
may have declined in light of recent
events, the lovers' rude disjunction—
though both untimely and indecent—
has little bearing on the cold,
hard, ancient stone that, through millennia,
has had the fortune to behold
the entrance and escape of many a
young couple, wanderer, plein-air
artiste—it's long since ceased to care.

2:51 pm

But, oh! What stories it could tell
were not its mouth sealed up with clay!
What legends prove, and myths dispel—
and what a marvellous array
of narratives and anecdotes
is printed deep within its stone!
Still ringing with the fading notes
and echoes of once-young, long-grown
and long-dead wanderers, it stores
the memories of generations.
Through floods, depressions, droughts and wars
a stream of constant visitations
has worn its stone almost as much
as miners' once-explosive touch.

2:54 pm

Most recently, it tells of two
now quite well-known. Its recollection
thus follows Glenn and Becca through
the early stages of affection,
as lovers more-or-less platonic,
exploring cliffs, rocks, and each other,
coaxing their half-formed, embryonic
affair, and careful not to smother
their passion's glowing, growing flame.
They scale the quarry walls, locate
retreats (which they are quick to claim
as theirs) and just appreciate
the welcome company and scenery,
lost among stone and splendid greenery.

2:57 pm

They find a rock which, from some angles,
looks just a little like an eagle,
soaring above the rocky tangles
strewn down below, majestic, regal.
They christen it the Eagle Rock,
acknowledging the shameless pun,
employing it henceforth, ad hoc:
to sit, relaxing, in the sun,
kissing, caressing, and conversing,
their passion growing stronger, denser,
closer—the tale now stops, reversing:
historian now acts as censor,
too chivalrous to kiss and tell
the secrets of its stony cell.

3:00 pm

So who could possibly predict
Glenn and Rebecca's fall from grace?
The Eagle now lies derelict,
the future site of no embrace,
no love, no joy, no understanding.
After its time of gleeful flight,
the eagle's well and truly landing—
no, crashing—sure as dynamite
would fell it to the quarry floor.
For how could it go on existing
after the lovers' premature
partition? Yet it does: resisting
the once-loved, now destructive force,
the rocks remain the same, of course.

3:03 pm

Even Glenn's crudely-chiselled scrawl—
a message of romance outdated—
remains embedded in the wall,
its text now unsubstantiated.
Within a more fantastic realm
the rock itself would fold and crack,
and mighty winds would overwhelm
the quarry, seeming to attack
and finally erase the text,
as severed by a mystic knife—
then calming, ready for the next
adventure. But in real life,
immune to such enchanted blasting,
it stays, unchanging, everlasting.

3:06 pm

Kris wakens for the second time
today. Immersed in soft, green-tinted
sunlight—ethereal, sublime—
her legs mysteriously printed
in intricate, cross-hatched relief
from lying on the grass too long,
much-needed sleep—the other thief
of time, seducing her with song
and silence—has already stolen
almost two hours of her day.
She stirs lethargically, eyes swollen
with recent slumber; shadows play
across her, and reflections probe
her body like a disco strobe.

3:09 pm

The air is noticeably cooler,
as afternoon removes the edge
from sunlight, the tyrannic ruler
of summer skies. The circling hedge
of parkland further insulates
against the heat; the searing swelter
slowly but surely dissipates
beneath the lush and living shelter
Kristin inhabits. Now she rises,
refreshed and only slightly drowsed,
and ready for new enterprises
to fill her afternoon: aroused
for fresh adventure, she decides
to meet the beach between its tides.

3:12 pm

The Bay tram leaves the city square,
where people clamber on and off,
where fountains gush dramatic, where
the homeless gather round to quaff
their bottles full of amber nectar.
Kris clatters down the aisle, procures
a ticket from a brusque inspector,
and sits back to enjoy the tour's
reputed scenery. The tram
is ancient, recollecting days
of old, when streetcars used to jam
the roads—though now, to paraphrase
one eager, tourist-minded driver,
'The Bay line is the sole survivor'.

3:15 pm

To pass her journey, Kris reflects
on everything she's seen and done
while in this country. She collects
reminders of each place—a tonne
of tickets, dockets and receipts,
brochures and postcards, bus timetables,
money and information sheets,
stamps, city maps and baggage labels
weighs down her backpack—but their witness
can't parallel the evidence
within her head: her mental fitness
is capable of huge, immense,
exhaustive, vivid, mental stores.
It's on this knowledge that she draws.

3:18 pm

The Gold Coast Highway; Hungry Jack's.
Whitsundays; Bi-Lo; barbecues.
The Sydney Opera House. *Mad Max*,
Mel Gibson. Daintree, kangaroos.
AC/DC. *This Sporting Life*.
Fat Cat. 'G'day mate!' Ridgey Didge.
Paul Hogan, crocs, 'That's not a knife.'
The reef. The Sydney Harbour Bridge.
Rolf Harris, and Dame Edna Everage.
Blue singlets. Wombats. 'Sic 'em, Rex!'
All kinds of alcoholic beverage:
Vic Bitter, Castlemaine XXXX.
Echidnas. 'Bloody!' Cooper's Light.
Shrimp. Violent Crumble. Vegemite.

3:21 pm

But while such an extensive list
of typical Australiana
is easily produced, she's missed—
through conscious act of will—a garner
of many locally available
things, objects, service, merchandise
in multitudes untold—unscalable—
with origins more imprecise,
which, from the northern hemisphere,
through emigration—or invasion—
have lately started to appear:
rogue elements in the equation
of localised economy,
supplanting native industry.

3:24 pm

McDonald's, Fuji, KFC.
Ford. Oprah Winfrey. Polaroid.
James Dean, KROQ, Bruce Lee.
'Twin Peaks'. Coke. Fleetwood Mac. Pink Floyd.
'Superman'; Sitcoms; fax machines.
IBM. 'Cheers'. 'Days of our Lives'.
Punk, rollerblades, *MAD* magazines.
Reebok. U2. Swiss army knives.
Minolta; pop-tarts; salad bars.
'Cool!' Baseball caps. Toyota. M*A*S*H.
Bill & Ted. AmEx. Gucci. Mars.
Basketball, Nike, plastic cash.
The Ninja Turtles. Sly Stallone.
Nintendo. Beach Boys. Ansafone.

3:27 pm

While not detracting from these things
themselves, she finds it somewhat boring
that each society now clings
tenaciously to this outpouring
of superpowers' exports. Such
conformity is lifeless, bland;
all memory of unique touch
is lost when any foreign land
embraces the forlorn banality
of keeping up with worldwide Joneses,
and sacred individuality
is sacrificed by these dull clones—is
it possible to keep one's pride
once singularity's denied?

3:30 pm

Kris doesn't think so. Disappointed
in Moscow, visiting Red Square,
to find that it had been anointed
with golden arches, her despair
grew steadily throughout her journey,
discovering that all the world
watched CNN, knew Bert and Ernie,
drank Pepsi. Litter trails unfurled,
traversing continents and seas,
the paper coffins of fast food
franchised worldwide—Kris followed these
with fast-decreasing gratitude,
convinced that she'd break down and bawl
if faced with one more shopping mall.

3:33 pm

The beachfront esplanade is teeming
with revellers as she arrives.
Though some say it's without redeeming
features, a bay subculture thrives
around its streets, along its sand.
A myriad of seaside food—
gelati, chips—is close at hand
across the road; a festive mood
infects the brisk and salty air.
The footpaths fill with folk attired
in towels and bathers, speakers blare
Madonna, tandem bikes are hired,
and seagulls stalk the seafront parks,
demanding tithes, like oligarchs.

3:36 pm

So, drenched in sun and atmosphere,
drinking in lemonade and life,
meandering along the pier,
enchanted by the breezy fife
of Neptune's piper, fed, well-rested,
enlivened by the damp, salt air,
she feels contented: unmolested
by duty, doubt, concern or care,
she's certain she could gladly walk
along the seafront and the sand
all day—eat ice-cream, sunbake, talk
to fishermen, enjoy the band—
and never think of getting bored,
responsibility ignored.

3:39 pm

With somewhat less untroubled ease,
Rebecca paces restlessly
through town: an urban Ulysses
condemned to roam the open sea
without respite, without relief.
Although she's wandered for a while
since leaving Glenn to tend his grief,
she still can't fully reconcile
her heart and mind in her decision:
the former just won't be persuaded
to acquiesce in love's division;
the latter, more the cynic, jaded
by time and reason, perseveres—
intolerant of mutineers.

3:42 pm

As if by instinct, she keeps moving,
afraid to stop, lest lack of action
bring painful thinking. Disapproving
of this irresolute reaction,
but powerless to intervene,
she travels like a lonely waif,
directionless and vague, between
the city limits, feeling safe
at present, fearful of the future
and also of the past, afraid
of no one but herself. 'The suture
to close this wound—my heart's first-aid—
will come with time,' she thinks. 'I hope.
But meanwhile, how am I to cope?'

3:45 pm

She finds herself back on the street
outside the café. Glenn's departed.
Imagining his glum retreat—
bewildered, beaten, broken-hearted—
she chokes, and has to hurry past,
averting eyes and mind. But, bravely,
she glances back until the blast
of memory subsides, then gravely
walks on, and feels more confident,
more capable, her fear replaced
with merely the desire to vent
her overwhelming feelings. Braced
and fortified, she goes to find
an ear in which to pour her mind.

3:48 pm

She finds Gus working at the pub
a little further up the road.
Though centred firmly at the hub
of several social scenes, now slowed
by daytime's dormancy—the still
before the storm—the place is quiet
and almost empty. At the till,
Gus feasts morosely on a diet
of takings, balance sheets and ledgers
to kill the time before the bar
brings students, poets, market hedgers
together, like a Shangri-La
attracting folk from left and right—
as happens every Friday night.

3:51 pm

'"Perhaps one day," you said,' Gus grins.
'Is that day—possibly—today?'
His quick evaluation wins
her trust. 'I'll happily allay
your curiosity,' she grants:
'Just be prepared for melodrama,
confusing angles, random slants,
philosophy...' 'The Dalai Lama
could hardly be more patient, Bec,'
he promises: 'No more excuses.
Just let me file this final cheque,
and then your ills are mine—what use is
a friend who's deaf to others' woes?'
'All right,' she answers. 'Here it goes...'

3:54 pm

As Bec goes on to tell her tale—
the third time since this morning—pressed
against the window is a pale,
dishevelled man. Unshaven, dressed
in army-surplus coat, he stands
outside the pub and smears the glass.
Gus sees his face and reprimands:
'Get out of here, Will! Move your arse!
You're not allowed here! Don't come back!'
The figure shrugs in resignation,
grimaces like a maniac
on some uncertain medication,
retreats, and disappears behind
the tinting—both from sight and mind.

3:57 pm

Will rounds a nearby corner, leaving
the bustle of the major road.
He finds the newfound hush relieving:
his senses are on overload
with so much restless agitation.
He far prefers a calmer scene,
infused with quiet inspiration—
unhurried, tranquil, still, serene.
For he's a poet, and his pen
works best when sheltered from intrusion,
describing themes beyond the ken
of mortals: tales of truth, illusion,
divinity, the buds of May—
that is, at least, until today.

4:00 pm

A figure on four legs appears
and bounds towards him. 'Zen!' he cries,
kneeling to scratch the shepherd's ears.
'How are you? What a glad surprise!
Where have you come from, girl?' He stands
in time to notice Ed and Art
approaching. Shaking both their hands
exultantly, Will says: 'My heart
is full—to see so many friends!
As flowers open to the rain,
so, too, my joyful soul ascends!'
'Always the poet,' Art says. 'Vain,
ornate, designed to overawe...'
Will shakes his head: 'Not any more.'

4:03 pm

Art's quizzical. 'Why? What's the matter?'
'There's no more magic,' Will exhales.
'The curse of poets in these latter,
too-modern times! The fairytales
are dead and gone, the fables spent.
The epic narratives of old—
Homer to Shakespeare—represent
the only stories ever told
that ever showed a novel flair;
we can but mimic those old days,
re-use their images, and share
their themes—once new, now all clichés.
The words are dead, and all the rhymes
have all been used a thousand times.

4:06 pm

'Just listen to a modern song—
the simple lyrics are unwavering—
attend the rhymes; before too long
you'll find the only couplets flavouring
their lines are endlessly repeated,
and so predictable—like 'girl'
and 'world'—the songsters all defeated
when trying to improve this pearl
of poetry! Like 'June', 'moon', 'spoon'!
'Above' and 'love'—or 'pretty', 'city'!
The words have all dried up too soon;
you can't put 'baby' in a ditty
and not use 'maybe' as its pair—
much to the lyricist's despair.

4:09 pm

'I've heard it said that all great plays—
and not-so-great ones, in addition—
can be reduced in simple ways
until each basic composition
is seen to be no more than one
of twenty-four or so synopses
from which more complex tales are spun.
Having conducted these autopsies
of plot and drama, evidently
imagination is restricted,
not infinite, and consequently
the ignoramus who predicted
that creativity would rule
forever was a blind old fool.'

4:12 pm

'Sorry to hear it,' Art consoles.
'The world has lost a great street poet.'
'That highfalutin rigmarole's
no good for me,' Will says. 'So stow it.
Don't pity me—I feel enlightened!
I've leapt from easy self-deception
to bitter truth, my senses heightened,
my mind now steeled against subreption.
Admittedly, I'm at a loss
regarding my next occupation,
but that's a bridge I'll have to cross
some other time—now, jubilation
pervades my soul, so newly rinsed
of lies!' He grins; Art's not convinced.

4:15 pm

Rebecca finishes her tale,
and sighs, 'Gus? What am I to do?
I thought I'd won, but doubts assail
my mind still now.' 'Bec, you'll pull through,'
Gus comforts. 'And, for what it's worth,
I think you took the only route
available. For why on earth
should you continue this pursuit
of worry, doubt and pain?' 'You're right.
Of course you are. I just don't need it.
Pour me a vodka, Gus. Tonight,
at last, I'm liberated, freed. It
just could have been no other way.
Get 'em before you're got, I say.'

4:18 pm

'It's every woman for herself,'
Gus offers. 'Get out while you can.
Just put this one back on the shelf
you call "experience"—the man
can handle it! And if he can't,
then better him than you. A cold
philosophy of life, I'll grant,
but nice guys finish last.' 'I'm sold,'
Rebecca tries to smile. 'I knew
you'd understand, and I'm so glad
you see it from my point of view.
My very own Sir Galahad—'
She pecks him quickly on the cheek—
'Thanks for your chivalrous critique.'

4:21 pm

She leaves the pub, her spirits lifted
at hearing her own views confirmed.
Her grinding, churning mind has shifted
into a low gear; though she's squirmed
unhappily beneath the weight
of bitter, chronic apprehension,
the pressure she's endured of late
is now no more. She feels the tension
dissolving from her neck and shoulders;
the death-cold fire that scorched so often,
now doused by freedom, dully smoulders.
Her heart's steel manacles now soften:
it spreads its wings, and rises, free,
at last rejoined with liberty.

4:24 pm

By contrast, Glenn presents a figure
bent under twice its normal load,
subjected to some frightful rigour,
some best-forgotten episode
of terror. Trudging up the drive
towards his house—a wounded bee
retreating to its deathbed hive,
a ruined, soulsick refugee—
he doesn't notice that the door
is open, kitchen light aglow,
and neither do his eyes explore
the carport, where a grey Volvo
sits though this morning there was none,
glittering in the falling sun.

4:27 pm

So Glenn is somewhat disconcerted
to find an unannounced intruder—
bespectacled, black-shoed, white-shirted—
frying a pan of barracuda,
a can of beer in his free hand,
as if Glenn's kitchen were his own.
Perplexed, Glenn doesn't understand
how, having lived for weeks alone,
a stranger stands before him now.
His daze lasts for a moment; then
the squatter turns around, his brow
raised in surprise, and offers, 'Glenn!
You want some fish? The best I've had!'
Glenn says, 'No, I'm not hungry, Dad.'

4:30 pm

'I couldn't get a flight tomorrow,'
the older man explains. 'They said—
in tones of poorly-studied sorrow—
I'd have to take today's instead,
or wait until next week. So here
I am again. The place looks great;
you've done a good job—though I fear
to look inside the cupboards, mate!
God only knows what I might find.'
Glenn shrugs away his jocularity:
'Dad, I've got something on my mind.
You can dispense with the hilarity,
and I'll be in my room.' 'Wait, son.
This time you're not the only one.'

4:33 pm

Glenn pauses, conscious of the tone
creeping into his father's voice—
an anguish that he's rarely known.
'When Mary died, I had no choice,'
the elder says. 'I had commitments:
contracts in Sydney, business clients;
I thought I'd sell the house, the fitments—
too many people had reliance
on me for me to stop and grieve.
And after that, I found relief
in constant work; I had to leave
her memory behind. In brief,
I ran away, and thought it cunning,
for these four years, to keep on running.

4:36 pm

'And so, for all this time, I've waited,
hoping the pain would disappear.
But it's not yet alleviated,
and I can't waste another year
pretending that I feel okay
when really I'm a wreck inside.
And that's why I intend to stay
at home from now on. I can't hide
or run—I tried, but just got tired,
and missed the things that really mattered.
Now that my energy's expired,
my shields and vain defences shattered,
I just want to be here for you,
and hope you'll be here for me too.'

4:39 pm

Glenn pauses. 'So that's why you left?
I know I never comprehended
your actions—why my world was cleft
time and again, from something splendid
into increasingly fragmented
debris of what was once complete.
An exodus unprecedented
saw those who shared my life retreat:
my parents, friends—what could I do
once they had gone? I missed you, Dad.
And all this time I never knew
whether the fugitive nomad
I called my parent would return
and show his fatherly concern.'

4:42 pm

'I missed you too, Glenn. I was weak.
You two were so alike, it's hard
to be with you—to hear you speak—
and still maintain the thin facade
that resolutely separates
dread memory from present thought.'
'But why forget?' Glenn remonstrates.
'Why would you bury and distort
her memory with such denial?
Why run away from what you loved?
This isn't business—you can't file
the past away; it won't be shoved
into a towering "Out" stack.'
'I know you're right. That's why I'm back.'

4:45 pm

There's no more need to verbalise
the thoughts that fly between the kin.
Tears well up in Glenn's father's eyes,
but still he wears a grateful grin,
relieved that he can now express
the pain that he'd so long rejected.
His features instantly confess
his sorrow to his son; connected
so firmly, no more words are needed
for Glenn to comfort and assuage:
verbosity is superseded
by their embrace as they engage
in fellowship long overdue,
creating one grief of their two.

4:48 pm

Fatigued by her perambulation,
Zoe decides to take a cab
back to her room. A dull deflation
envelops her; her gift of gab,
absent without official leave,
has left her feeling dull and tired.
The taxi grants a brief reprieve—
'Where to, ma'am?'—and she feels inspired,
as in all times of slender hope,
when any straw at hand seems clutchable.
Reaching the limit of her rope,
tactics she would have thought untouchable
are all she has now. 'Driver? Take
me somewhere good, for heaven's sake.'

4:51 pm

The cabbie looks a little quizzical.
'I'm sorry, lady? A location?
An address—nothing metaphysical:
it's been a long, hot day.' 'Damnation
to weather, time and news reports!'
Zo cries. 'I've walked around all day,
and trying times take last resorts.
So if you'd please be on your way—'
She pauses—'I'd be most indebted.'
The driver turns and pulls a face
as if detecting something fetid,
but throws his cab in gear to chase
the amber lights, and is soon cruising
for what his passenger fears losing.

4:54 pm

'You're not from round here, ma'am. The States?'
Despite his scowl, he can't resist
the cabbie's code, which legislates
no opportunity be missed
that might result in conversation—
or, more correctly, monologue.
'New York, yes.' 'Then your emigration
doesn't surprise me! Too much smog,
and crime—not safe to walk the streets!
As cities go, it's just too big.
Too many people. Sure, it beats
your Hicksville, USA—a pig
wouldn't consent to live there—but...'
He talks as Zoe's eyes slide shut.

4:57 pm

Kris, midway through a pink gelati,
is startled as a sudden cry
rings through the crowd in tones of hearty
familiarity. 'July—
the Stockholm hostel, right? You're Kris!'
She turns and sees a young, white man
approaching. 'Jesus! Isn't this
some weird coincidence! I ran
from over there—I saw you...' He's
a traveller (his clothes betray him),
and moves with confidence and ease,
as if no trouble could waylay him...
Kris cringes as she recognises
the bearer of these far surprises.

5:00 pm

His name is Todd. As he divulged,
they shared a hostel in Stockholm.
Alone and lonely, they indulged
in conversation: polychrome
discussions in the common room
of travel stories, revelations
of home life told with distant gloom,
opinions, free associations
and jokes combining to acquaint
the strangers. He called home Chicago,
and Christopher, the patron saint
of travellers, had kept his cargo
protected and himself alive
three or four months—or maybe five.

5:03 pm

Just shy of Kristin's twenty years,
he proved a fine short-term companion,
until a night replete with beers
and tales of fjords and the Grand Canyon
in one of Stockholm's downtown bars.
When finally emerging, poorer
in health and wealth, beneath the stars
and slowly flickering aurora,
arms intertwined for both support
and friendship, voices somewhat slurred,
laughing at nothing—drunk—a thought
in Kristin's mind abruptly stirred,
filling her with a sudden fright:
her comrade's grip was much too tight.

5:06 pm

She tried to move, but couldn't. Stopping,
he circled, and a firm embrace
made her his captive. Twisting, hopping,
she struggled as he touched her face
and planted an unwanted kiss
against her lips. He seemed surprised
at her resistance: 'Isn't this
what you were after?' he chastised,
thrusting his hand beneath her shirt,
fumbling ineptly with her bra,
holding her arms so hard they hurt,
pushing her up against a car—
and then, retreating from the sound
of its alarm, against the ground.

5:09 pm

On top of her, he forced her knees
apart and reached toward her dress,
slurring 'So hard to get? You tease...'
and managing one last caress
before his bloodstream alcohol
hit critical and he collapsed
unconscious, like a raggy doll,
too lagered, burgundied and schnappsed
for anything but quiet snoring.
Kris crawled from under him, disgusted,
her righteous fury overawing.
Thinking 'He seemed so well-adjusted,'
she fixed her clothes, went home, and kept
her thoughts at bay until she slept.

5:12 pm

The next day she checked out at dawn,
tiptoeing past his dorm in case
some spirit rescuer had borne
him from the site of their disgrace
and he lay, calmly catatonic,
to soon awake and wonder what
he'd done to ruin their platonic
relationship, an opaque blot
obscuring last night's recollection
and making its events seem inky,
eclipsed. Kris made the boat connection
transporting her to far Helsinki,
leaving her undesired escort
behind for good—or so she thought.

5:15 pm

Remembering, Kris turns away.
Todd cries, 'No, wait! Let me explain...
I'm sorry! I was drunk, okay?'
But all excuses are in vain:
she hisses, 'Stay away from me!
How dare you—' 'Look, I meant no harm...
I wouldn't—couldn't!—honestly...'
He reaches out and grips her arm
to keep her close; her body trembles
to feel the pressure of the hand
that so unbearably resembles
her old assault. She can't withstand
this contact with the man she shuns,
so, breaking free, she turns and runs.

5:18 pm

He's after her. She seeks the crowds,
darting between their ambling figures,
hoping to hide behind their shrouds
of anonymity—these rigours
hardly deter him from pursuit,
so, bent on fleet-of-foot escape,
she calculates a different route
demanding that she deftly scrape
through winding side-streets, narrow alleys
and unexpected corners. Dropping
behind a moment, he soon rallies
and closes on her—now his stopping
seems ever more remote a hope:
she won't evade his loathsome grope.

5:21 pm

'Look, what's your problem, anyhow?'
he gasps when reaching shouting distance.
'Nobody these days takes a vow
of chastity—why your resistance?'
Kris answers with an added spurt
of speed and energy, outpacing
any attempt he might exert
to emulate her frantic racing.
Instead, he pants: 'Look, I'm a guy
and you're a girl—where does it say
that anyone can't have a try?
So what's the matter? Are you gay,
queer, lesbian—like girls, do you?'
Kris cries, 'Well, so what if I do?'

5:24 pm

Her answer stops him in his tracks,
and, seizing on the opportunity
to head off any more attacks,
she scrambles to secure immunity
through further maze-like twists and turns,
first sprinting, later jogging, strolling,
meandering. Her stomach churns
with fear and anger, but consoling
herself that, since she's won the chase,
the day can hold no more surprises,
her heart resumes its resting pace—
until she turns and realises
that though she's free at last, the cost
is such that she's completely lost.

5:27 pm

The beach lies to the city's west,
beyond the massive tracts of sprawling
suburbs, where petty bourgeois rest
in houses they insist on calling
'Arcadia' or 'Avalon',
the mass-produced and uniform
encampments of the eidolon
of wealth where there is none, aswarm
with forged material possessions—
plated with gold, but lead inside.
This edifice of first impressions
and borrowed guises tries to hide
its shameful secrets from its neighbours—
but isn't foolproof in its labours.

5:30 pm

But in the south, the gentle hills
disrupt the city's rigid map
and thin the housing sprawl that fills
the suburbs, threatening to wrap
the world in concrete and red brick.
Accompanying altitude
is greenery that grows more thick
along the valleys that intrude
between the hills and ribboned roads,
the metropolitan expansion
reduced to thinly-spread abodes
perching in places no McMansion
could venture—enemies of gravity
in attitudes of genteel suavity.

5:33 pm

Glenn's father lives in such a house,
built by an architect he knew
from college to protect his spouse
and unborn son—who quickly grew—
approaching twenty years ago.
He stands within its kitchen now,
recovering from waves of woe
he never thought he might allow.
Glenn's with him. 'Dad, there's something more,'
he says. 'You must have met Rebecca,
my girl—the point is kind of sore;
I feel as though a double-decker
has come up from behind and thumped me
across the street—that is, she dumped me.'

5:36 pm

'I'm sorry, son. This doesn't seem
to be our day. So what's the story?
You held her in such high esteem...'
'Don't ask me. Things were hunky-dory
until today—and then she left.
Some muddled riddle of distress,
confusion, anguish... hardly deft
or eloquent, I must confess—
I didn't see her point at all.
She felt exposed and unprotected—
against what, though, I can't recall—
and says it's *me* who has affected
her in this disappointing manner:
so now my works have felt her spanner.'

5:39 pm

'I understand how you must feel,
but maybe try to comprehend
how she feels, too...' 'Oh, Dad, be real!
We menfolk can, at best, pretend
to penetrate the female mind—
their thoughts are of a different fashion.'
'A slanted view of womankind,
and quite untrue. Where's your compassion?
Don't others think the same as you?
We all seek happiness, fear pain,
and try to reconcile the two
effectively, and so remain
within the sphere of shaky sanity
we tentatively call humanity.

5:42 pm

'It's easy to mistake the odds
and overestimate the risk
of failure and defeat. The gods
themselves may fear a basilisk
and think it best not to torment it—'
'All right,' growls Glenn: 'My ego's bruised
already—do you have to dent it
further?' His father looks confused;
Glenn struggles to explain: 'It's just
that if I'm such a dull reward
that she won't acquiesce to trust
my constancy... I'm not a fraud!
I'd not betray her! Can't she see?'
'You should be telling her, not me.'

5:45 pm

Glenn pauses. 'You know what? You're right.
I'll find her—talk to her—convince her
that I'm for real, and reignite
the flame that's sputtered weakly since her
unfortunate attack of flighty
uneasiness and trepidation.
I'll raise the ghost of Aphrodite,
relieve her doubt and consternation,
and harmony will be restored.
The swirling mistral of her fear
is no match for my shining sword,
which slices through the stratosphere,
delivering true light where bleakness
gives rise to cowardice and weakness.'

5:48 pm

‘I don’t know what we’re doing here,’
Zo mutters as she trudges quickly
across the grass. ‘Was I unclear?
I said a *good* place, not this sickly
and uninspiring vacant lot.
There’s graveyards all around the world,
and I can guarantee they’ve got
more famous tenants than those curled
six feet beneath these worn old stones.
Vienna boasts Beethoven, Brahms
and Mozart; Stratford holds the bones
of Shakespeare; Père Lachaise
embalms Jim Morrison, Wilde, Molière—
how can this paltry plot compare?’

5:51 pm

‘Enough of tedious comparisons,’
the cabbie growls. ‘I’m sure you’ve viewed
celebrities in ghostly garrisons
across the globe, but quietude
is now required: be still, and see.’
She does. They’re in a small necropolis
of broken stone and twisted tree
some distance from the main metropolis.
Across the uncut grass are strewn
lopsided and time-weathered graves
marked in the alphabet of rune
and unknown sign; loose gravel paves
a narrow path between the tombs
that spread beneath in catacombs.

5:54 pm

'Now, take a closer look,' instructs
the taxi driver: 'Be respectful.'
He points his finger and conducts
her gaze: a stone which, through neglectful
decades, is now completely blank,
anonymously sits before them.
'So simple—subtle—yet so frank,'
the cabbie muses. 'Can't ignore them.
Reminders of our own mortality.
This stone, effaced and empty, twisted
by inescapable finality,
as if no person had existed
to carve a name and date—too shallow!—
into this rock, which now lies fallow.'

5:57 pm

'Is this a *What's it all about*
soliloquy?' Zo interjects.
'For—no offence—I kind of doubt
we'll satisfy our intellects
or find the answers carved in stone
in this old place.' 'No—no more speeches.
Wait here. I want to be alone
for just a minute,' he beseeches.
Wandering off, he takes some flowers
from one sepulchre and transplants
them nearby, where grey stone embowers
another memory; he chants
a line in Latin on this shrine
and doffs his hat to auld lang syne.

6:00 pm

Zoe, indignant of exclusion,
creeps up behind him as he stands,
oblivious to her intrusion,
in thoughtful silence, eyes closed, hands
clasped regally behind his back.
'Who's this?' she whispers. Without turning,
he answers, 'It's my daughter, Jacq—
for Jacqueline. A most discerning
young lady, who I'm sure you'd like;
she dreamed of acting in New York.
She's been here ten years. Rode her bike
into a car—I come to talk
and listen every now and then...
to visit my tragedienne.

6:03 pm

'She'd be eighteen. I sometimes wonder
what she'd be doing—who she'd be—
if fortune hadn't trapped her under
this rock. At university?
Perhaps she'd study architecture.
She might have seen the world already...
written a novel. I conjecture
a future for her full of heady
experience, and wealth, and fame,
and happiness—but I'd be glad
of any future: it's the same
to me if she were Queen of Chad
or on the dole—I wouldn't care,
provided that I had her there.'

6:06 pm

He pauses, leaving Zo to feel—
after her scathing cynicism—
so absolute and pure a heel
she wishes some great cataclysm
would rend the earth beneath her feet
and pull her under. 'Yes, I'm sure
she would have had a life complete
with all those things,' she says, demure
and humbled. 'And one, greater thing:
a father who believed in her.
She'd value him above her King
of Chad, I know. So thank you, sir.
this is—though hidden, peaceful, quiet—
a special place; I can't deny it.'

6:09 pm

A motley cohort roams the streets
back in the city: poor but proud,
they wear their glad rags like the pleats
of any uniform. Their loud
exchange is heard from far around
as they engage in dialogue:
the raucous and anarchic sound
of three men and a barking dog,
a boisterous invading army
with no regard for the affairs
of those opposing their tsunami
of rags and merriment, confrères
as close as any Musketeers—
companions, colleagues, partners, peers.

6:12 pm

'It's Friday night,' says Arthur. 'What
are we to do to celebrate?'
'A party in a vacant lot?'
Ed offers. 'Drink, and stay up late?'
'We do that every night,' says Art.
'That proves that it's a good idea!'
cries Ed, triumphant. 'So, let's start.
You bring the wine; I'll find some beer.'
Zen barks, but Arthur says: 'Sit tight.
This is a singular occasion—
the longest day, the shortest night,
according to some old equation—
a special evening. So I'm thinking
we'll mark it better by *not* drinking.'

6:15 pm

'You're very quiet,' Ed observes
of Will. 'Perhaps you've got suggestions?'
'My own profundity innerves
me more than your moronic questions,'
Will answers. 'I'm immersed in thought,
so don't disturb me for a minute.'
('I wonder what he's thinking?' 'Nought—
his head's big, but there's nothing in it,'
Eddie and Art exchange, aside.)
The sometime poet's furrowed brow
reveals a study dignified
and rigorous, which will allow
no rest until this solemn seeker
is satisfied... Will cries, 'Eureka!'

6:18 pm

The other two are startled by
the poet's sudden exclamation.
His mouth is open wide; his eye
is gleaming bright with inspiration
and maybe madness. 'Guys! I've found it!'
he cries. 'I've been blind—all the while
I've stumbled sightlessly around it,
but missed it—barely—by a mile!'
'One second, Archimedes,' Art
attempts to chasten. 'We're dismayed.
Reverse a minute, and impart
the meaning lost in your charade.
What does your reverie endorse?'
Will halts. 'Why, poetry, of course!

6:21 pm

'I told you that the classic themes
and images had all been used—
their reservoirs exhausted, streams
run dry and dusty—and accused
the poet of finite invention,
limited range. And this is true.
But hidden from my comprehension
was something that I always knew:
that while grand epics of pomposity
and noble deed grow quickly stale—
repeated, clichéd—this monstrosity
is spared from the more simple tale
of unassuming actuality
that poets, scathing, dub reality.

6:24 pm

'Reflect on this: our inspiration—
since we are human, and thus frail—
suffers from natural retardation;
the flights of fancy that assail
our minds are from a finite store,
and soon exhausted. Whereas forces
like nature, destiny, the law
of physics, chance and fate are sources
of truly infinite variety.
The complex pressures they exert
on landscape, history, society—
on life—give rise to tales unhurt
by limits plaguing our creation:
they're greater than imagination.

6:27 pm

'You see, the answer doesn't lie
in magical and grand allusions,
but in the life that passes by
all people: in the doubts, confusions,
simplicities and lowly deeds
of common folk who go about
their lives, fulfilling human needs,
existing day to day without
concern regarding plots and themes.
In scenery, in social functions,
in worldly hopes and simple dreams,
choices, decisions and compunctions
regarding these. The subject's plain:
the poetry of the mundane.'

6:30 pm

'I get it,' Ed, enthusiastic,
joins in: 'You know, I never cared
for highfalutin and bombastic
expression. I was always scared
of "wherefore art thou", "thy" and "thee",
and "haveth", "giveth", "loseth", "saith"—
those things all just confusedeth me!
I always had a lot more faith
in what I witnessed every day—
my cans, that building there, that man
who bends balloons...' 'That alleyway!'
Art joins. 'That tourist from Japan!
And look! A lyric verse full-blown:
that woman on the telephone.'

6:33 pm

Rebecca slouches, not suspecting
her newly-found poetic status,
against a public phone, projecting
hope and despair as each hiatus
between the ringing signals mounts
into an ever-longer stretch
of silence, ominous. She counts
twelve rings before her efforts fetch
an answer; verging on surrender,
she jumps, and says, 'Oh, Fred? That you?
It's me—your juvenile offender—
I'm still at large! No, that's untrue...
they couldn't prove a thing! It's good
to hear you're in the neighbourhood...'

6:36 pm

As she goes on, her voice, and stance,
and aspect become subtly changed,
and both contraction and expanse
possess her features. Rearranged
this way, she seems much more at ease,
experienced and in control:
at once as wise as Socrates,
as tactical as Charles de Gaulle;
alluring as a siren, witty
as Lear's fool, mischievous as Puck,
as cool as Bogart's Rick, and pretty
as Aphrodite, with the pluck
of Artemis—there's little doubt
she's stronger for this turnabout.

6:39 pm

'How long's it been, Fred, since we split?
A year or so? You went to Perth,
remember—so we had to quit!
Can't follow you around the earth,
cute as you are... what? No, it's true!
But seeing as you're back in town...
you read my mind! That's something you
could always do. Yeah... upside-down,
that's how you knew me. Once or twice!—'
She laughs—'So, I was thinking, now
that you've returned, it might be nice
to take up where we left off. How
would you like meeting me tonight?
The pub... same one. At eight, all right?'

6:42 pm

Kristin's been lost before. She'd rather
meander aimlessly around—
even if this means walking farther—
than be peremptorily bound
to meekly follow any map:
if she can help it, she won't buy one.
This often proves a handicap,
as instincts constantly defy one
when one is in a foreign setting:
the sea is in a new direction,
the sun misplaced, and Kris, forgetting
to make the requisite correction
for this new, nether hemisphere,
finds intuition less than clear.

6:45 pm

The suburbs marching slowly past
fade to homologous expanses,
the slums of a restricted caste
determined mainly by finances.
The houses blur, becoming patches
of decorator colour; lawns
and gardens are reduced to snatches
of green and brown. As Kristin mourns
her lost direction, this non-focus—
impressionistic pointillism
issuing from her unknown locus,
diffracted wildly through the prism
of terror and confusion—grows
malevolent and bellicose.

6:48 pm

The normally dull, unobtrusive
identikit brick bungalows
become alarmingly abusive,
arranged in military rows,
in classic tactical formation.
The streets are grimy with decay,
disease and slow dilapidation:
not an attractive place to stray
unknowingly within at all.
Even the sun, which gently bathes
in gold as it begins to fall,
seems cold, bereft of life—it swathes
the world in damp, oppressive fear—
too harsh, too clinical and clear.

6:51 pm

She lifts her pace as she proceeds,
not certain where she's headed, but
increasingly aware she needs
to be elsewhere, and fast. Her strut
becomes more desperate as she worries
how late the public transport runs
and when the shops will close; she hurries
still faster as she sees the sun's
descending and expanding disc
growing more orange—truly scared
of dealing with the added risk
of finding herself unprepared
and lost upon these streets at night,
she runs, her heels lent wings by fright.

6:54 pm

Glenn labours to articulate
his state of thinking by contriving
to re-establish his ornate
and epic graphic tale, reviving
the characters and plots and themes
for one last, ultimate adventure.
The change in circumstance now deems
it politic that the indenture
against the tale's continuation—
implied in an ornate 'The End'—
should be abandoned: annexation
is necessary to amend
the story now so incomplete,
intolerably obsolete.

6:57 pm

He tries to sketch Rebecca, cast
back in her role of leather-clad,
barbaric figure of the past.
But this time an expression mad
and dangerous invades her face.
With friendship treacherously feigned
and lavishly affected grace
she thrusts her two-edged blade, blood-stained
and sinister, straight through the heart
of our raw, unsuspecting hero—
a poor exchange for Cupid's dart.
Leaving him cold and pale as Pierrot,
his body robbed of blood and pneuma,
she laughs with grim, triumphant humour.

7:00 pm

The trouble is, Glenn's hand is numb,
and what his mind attempts to conjure
is lost—as if some fiend had come
and exorcised it with a plunger
before it had a chance to find
its way to paper. It's as though
his inner eye's been rendered blind,
and severed nerves distort the flow
of impulses toward his pen:
he's left to scrawl in esoteric
illegibility. His yen
to vent his feelings grows hysteric,
frustrated by this inability,
this tragic mental infertility.

7:03 pm

Impotent, powerless, denied
the reassuring transformation
of cold reality to wide,
fantastic, safe imagination,
Glenn finds himself without escape
and consequently without hope.
Without the faculty to shape
the staggering kaleidoscope
of real life into a form
more tractable, he's lost, exposed
and naked in the raging storm
of overwhelming fact—cold, closed
to reinterpretation, hard:
impossible to disregard.

7:06 pm

And so, since his retreat is blocked,
his only option is attack.
He's been attempting to concoct
a scheme to win Rebecca back—
sound arguments and strong persuasions,
appeals to memory, recourse
to happiness in past occasions.
His present troubles reinforce
his dedication and conviction
that there can be no other option
for neutralising his affliction.
Assured that with this plan's adoption
there'll be no cause to be depressed,
he goes to put it to the test.

7:09 pm

Perched on the fourteenth floor, Zo sits
before her portable PC,
delivering a frenzied blitz
against each wildly clacking key.
A jug of hot room-service brew
provides caffeine invigoration,
and sugar substitute—in lieu
of calories—in concentration
near-lethal also serves to speed
her mind into a paroxysm
of creativity. Indeed,
her current mental anarchism
might cause the keys to overheat—
especially that marked 'Delete'.

7:12 pm

She writes: *This sleepy country town*
admittedly boasts few attractions
for travellers who wish to drown
their boredom in the stupefactions
of wondrous, vibrant, foreign cities.
This journalist—who, having seen
Rio, Bangkok and Paris, pities
anywhere lauded as 'serene'—
has stumbled on no new, exciting
or stimulating claims to fame
or fortune at the time of writing.
In fact, it's tempting to disclaim
the whole place as a non-event:
a futile city to frequent...

7:15 pm

'Not a good start,' Zo thinks, deleting
the paragraph with two key-presses.
'That peevish, discontented bleating
is not my plan.' She retrogresses
back to the top-left of the screen
and starts again: *Although I've found*
this city to be calm, serene
and with no power to astound
on any of the more traditional
criteria, it must be said
that it possesses some additional,
significant aspect instead:
some inexpressible, abstract
je ne sais quoi—vague, inexact.

7:18 pm

'Too vague and inexact by half,'
Zoe adjudges as she wipes
this latest effort with a laugh
empty of humour. 'Archetypes
are what we need—concrete examples,
not cloudy castles in the air.'
She tries once more: *Among the samples*
of speciality and flair
that typify this unique place
are oddly-vested street musicians,
folks who prefer a languid pace,
morose young men, and expeditions
to graveyards full of tragic stories
and cabbies with memento moris.

7:21 pm

She checks this over and concedes:
'That doesn't make much sense at all.
and anyway, "unique flair" reads
far too exuberant. I'd call
it, rather, "boring", "faintly weird"
or "dull". I'd better tone it down.'
She does: *Initially, I feared*
reporting on this backwoods town.
Museums, galleries, containing
repetitive and tired displays
I'd never found too entertaining
even in naive, younger days
were all I dared hope to expect.
And, basically, I was correct.

7:24 pm

'And now I'm back where I began,'
she cries aloud, exasperated.
'I'm sure that an orang-utan
could write a more sophisticated
report by punching random keys!
God knows I'm trying, but I just
can't exercise my journalese
on this assignment—I'm nonplussed
trying to make the language fit
hell-paving but sincere intention!
No matter what I scribble, it
consists of either condescension
or grievous, unprovoked assault...
which surely can't be all my fault.'

7:27 pm

Since she can't sate her appetite
for literary composition,
feeling an artless neophyte
she mounts a baser expedition
to slake a more compliant thirst.
Some dinner, and perhaps a drink,
would help. She takes the lift to first:
her innards rise, but spirits sink,
descending from her room like Zeus
from high Olympus. When she stops
she finds herself before Chez Bruce,
the hotel restaurant, where chops,
steak, chips and other haute cuisine
are served with bread and margarine.

7:30 pm

The pub's become a good deal busier
as Bec walks once more through its doors.
Drinkers debate whose beer is fizzier;
spilt alcohol anoints the floors
with sticky puddles. All the benches
are filled with hearty, raucous folk
like Viking warriors and wenches,
laughing at some half-mumbled joke,
quaffing their lagers with abandon.
Musicians tune their tools out back,
and people look for things to stand on
to rise above the growing pack
of revellers—to be denounced
by angry staff, and outward-bounced.

7:33 pm

'I think you've got a crush on me,'
Gus shouts above the background static
of ribaldry and repartee.
'What are you, some sort of fanatic?
Why else attend this godforsaken
abyss? You've tailed me since this morning.
But listen, I'm already taken!'
Rebecca laughs: 'Thanks for the warning,
but this time I'm not here for you.
I'm meant to meet a friend at eight.'
'You're early.' 'Nothing else to do,'
Rebecca shrugs: 'He won't be late.'
'Well, I can't hang around. This throng
think they've been waiting far too long.'

7:36 pm

She leaves him to his task of pouring
the masses' drinks, and sees a group
of uni friends who, with adoring
expressions of elation, whoop
their greetings. She returns these gladly,
raising her hand and shouting, 'Liz!
Felicity! Kym! Marvin! Bradley!'—
but doesn't move from where she is,
for through the doorway Fred appears,
as strangers enter town saloons
in western movies from the years
of Butch and Sundance. Becca swoons
convincingly at her outlaw,
and calls 'Hey, over here! Yee-haw!'

7:39 pm

'Hey, little lady,' Fred replies.
'I ain't seen you around these parts
of late—your call was some surprise.
What you been doing?' 'Breaking hearts,'
Rebecca answers: 'Welcome back.'
They kiss self-consciously, restrained
at first, then with an utter lack
of apprehensiveness, detained
by no reserve, no doubt, no caution—
two individuals combined,
faces compressed in strange distortion,
tongues, lips and bodies intertwined:
a living, breathing billet-doux.
Fred says, 'Uh-huh. I missed you too.'

7:42 pm

'What do you want to drink?' Bec asks.
'I'll shout you one for your homecoming.'
'Rye whiskey from the meanest casks,'
is Fred's reply: 'But if we're slumming
tonight, I guess I'll have a beer.'
'You got it. Beer, that is.' She plunges
gallantly through a wild frontier
of borderers, all soaked as sponges,
and fights for access to the bar.
'What, you again?' Gus shouts above
the clamour: 'This is quite bizarre.'
Rebecca grins. 'My friend would love
a beer, he says, and I'd not mind
some bourbon, if you'd be so kind.'

7:45 pm

'For seven dollars, I can be
the pinnacle of benefaction,'
he answers, pouring: 'Bonhomie,
philanthropy, unselfish action...
you name it—it can all be bought
with currency or credit. Here,
your drinks. Allow me to extort
the charge for this benignant beer
and—bourbon? Kind of hardish-core
for daylight drinking, surely?' 'Is
interrogation part of your
job-spec these days?' says Bec: 'Don't quiz
me like you were my worried mother—
just be prepared to pour another.'

7:48 pm

'Your money's wish is my command,'
says Gus, a little mercenarily.
'It's not my place to reprimand.
I mean, there's nothing necessarily
improper about drinking highly
intoxicating, potent brews
that might affect—' 'Oh, cut the wily
psychology! You can't refuse
to serve me, Gus—you're a bartender,
for heaven's sake!' 'That doesn't mean
that I'm no longer a defender
of ladies' honour.' 'Have I been
a lady, ever, since you've known me?
Now's not the moment to enthrone me.'

7:51 pm

'I wouldn't dream of such a thing.
Be careful, though, is all I'm saying.
This stuff can pack a nasty sting,
as I've discovered by surveying
the aftermath of people drinking
when they're emotional, like you.'
'Give me a break, Gus! I'm not sinking
my sorrows—I'm not even blue.
It's just a drink, you know. It's social.'
'I've seen the outcome. You'd not guess
they came into the bar precocial,
given the way they end up.' 'Yes,
but they were them, and I am me.
I'm in control, so let me be.'

7:54 pm

'Hey, Gus! Don't you enjoy your job?'
a waitress shouts across the bar,
attempting to assuage the mob
that's gathered in a reservoir
of angry and impatient punters
during the latter conversation.
'If not, I'm sure a dozen juntas
would revel in your resignation.
I hear the local crisis centre
is always after volunteers
if you're so passionate to enter
the social-worker's role. Arrears
remain outstanding here, though, so
just serve these folks and you can go.'

7:57 pm

'Don't be a bitch, okay? I'm busy,'
Gus shouts, indignantly maligned.
'Has bar-work got you in a tizzy?
Can't handle it? I'm sure you'll find
that unemployment's far less stressful.'
'She's right, you know,' Rebecca shrugs.
'This argument's quite unsuccessful.
You pour the multitudes their mugs
of comfort; I'll go back to Fred;
we'll all be happy.' She retreats
in the direction aforesaid:
Fred's found a pair of vacant seats,
which, in this place of many oddities,
are rare and coveted commodities.

8:00 pm

Deep in the central railway station—
a huge, sky-reaching, high-roofed hall
fed by a parallel formation
of metal tracks along which crawl
the stubby silver-orange worms
delivering their human cargo
like patient, plodding pachyderms—
Arthur discusses his embargo
on drinking beer tonight with Ed.
'You must admit that you'd prefer
a visit to the beach instead—
let's leave these wearisome milieux
behind us, and propose a toast
to celebration on the coast.'

8:03 pm

Will's gone off to appreciate
the lyric poetry contained
within signs reading *Leaves Track Eight*
at 9:15, so Ed's ordained
to speak for both himself and friend.
'Yeah, sure, whatever,' he concedes.
'But, north or south?' 'I'd recommend
a southern beach to meet our needs,'
Arts says. 'The sunset's always better,
although the wind's a little harsher,
and last time I was there I met a
vendor of cut-price victuals: Marsha,
she's called. It's perfect, can't you see?'
Eddie says, 'Yes, your majesty.'

8:06 pm

The train's reflective silver siding
glows orange with the setting sun.
Art and his colleagues are sent riding
towards the multimegaton
nuclear holocaust in space—
fervent in fission and in fusion—
as if engaging in a race
against the everyday illusion
of its decay and disappearance.
The sky is marked with coloured streaks
of atmospheric interference—
an astral face with flushing cheeks;
an artist's palette, sometime filled
with pastels, overturned and spilled.

8:09 pm

Thin bands of cloud, electrified
by sunset into neon strips
of red and shining orange, glide
across the sky like woolly ships
traversing oceans set afire
with molten, hot, volcanic lava.
Above, an astronomic choir
brings forth a shimmering ottava
of colour as opposed to sound:
a symphony of reds, sonata
of oranges—hues never found
elsewhere, in smoothly blended strata
of scarlet, ochre, lemon, jade,
lilac, and every other shade.

8:12 pm

The circle of our nearest star
grows gibbous as it slowly drops
towards the earth: an avatar
who—some would say unwisely—swaps
its heavenly address for one
upon the humble ground. Descending
gradually out of sight, the sun
bejewels the sea with its impending
destruction, casting golden ripples
from the horizon to the shore
in dancing, many-coloured stipples
glittering like a disco floor,
or like a path of living light
between the daytime and the night.

8:15 pm

The falling sphere becomes immersed
in water, threatening to boil
the seas with its triumphant burst
of final, moribund turmoil.
Oceans burn orange as the sliver
of sunlight slowly sinks and drowns,
and up and down the world a shiver
acknowledges Apollo's crown's
been toppled, and its dark usurper
is shrouding half the world in robes
of blackness. Guided by the sherpa
Diana—smaller of the globes
among the heavenly elite—
the night arrives on stealthy feet.

8:18 pm

High in spirits—and on them too—
Rebecca laughs as she regresses
back to the front bar. 'Hey! Renew
my glasses, tender!' she addresses
the flustered form that Gus presents.
He turns, and signals *wait a minute.*
'Can't talk at all now,' he laments
while serving her. 'You'll land me in it!'
'Well, no complaints—we're doing fine.'
'I only wonder what Glenn thinks!'
'He doesn't star in my design—
we've severed our ill-fated links.'
Gus cocks his head towards the door,
and says, 'I wouldn't be so sure.'

8:21 pm

Glenn's figure in the doorway pauses,
scanning the bustle of the room
near-sightedly. His presence causes
Becca to hastily resume
her journey back to Fred's two chairs,
where she slumps down as if in hiding,
catching Fred somewhat unawares:
'You told me you were law-abiding
these days,' he says. 'Are you in trouble?'
'Don't turn around—' Fred promptly does.
'—You idiot! You want to double
my worries?' 'He can't be the fuzz—
too young! What is he, undercover?'
'No—worse than that. He's my ex-lover.'

8:24 pm

'I thought I'd find you here,' says Glenn.
'I've been all up and down the street
attempting to locate your den.'
'Congratulations—how discreet
of you,' Bec says, a touch sarcastic.
'Oh, hurl discretion to the wind,'
Glenn answers: 'If I must use drastic
measures in order to rescind
this rank injustice, then so be it.'
'Look, what's your problem, anyway?'
'It's both of ours, and we can't flee it—'
'I fled it earlier today,
and you should too. Go take a walk.'
'I can't. I came in here to talk.

8:27 pm

'For one, I know just how you're feeling.
I may be male, but still I've learned
a thing or two. So your concealing
emotions that you don't want burned
is no great mystery to me.
I sympathise—I feel your pain,
your doubt, and your uncertainty.
But in the war of heart and brain,
there's only one consistent winner.
Can mental process rule emotion?
Although I'm only a beginner,
I've found that even true devotion
to rationality can't quell
that seething sentimental swell.

8:30 pm

'I also recognise the risk
you take when you entrust your soul
to someone. Like an odalisque—
a slave of love—you find your whole
existence hangs upon the thread
of their approval and ongoing
devotion. I know why you fled—
how could I not? Your fear is showing—
but I think we're a risk worth taking.
No victory exists without
the possibility of breaking
into an unheroic rout—
defeat's the risk that makes success
worth any level of duress.'

8:33 pm

'I'm sure that I appreciate
the pep-talk,' says Rebecca coolly.
'But I'm afraid you're just too late.
Your gung-ho call to arms is duly
noted, but I just can't subscribe
to such a suicidal plan
of battle. Though your Zulu tribe
or crazy kamikaze clan
might revel in the opportunity
to chance the odds—to show their bravery
relying on the vague impunity
of rushing fools—it's quite unsavoury
to my mind, which, as you've observed,
admittedly is more reserved.'

8:36 pm

'I'm not suggesting you should take
a wholly unpropitious chance—
especially with so much at stake.
Forgive me if I might advance
the notion that our tragic fate
is *not* inevitably sealed,
but is still free to deviate
from that direction you've revealed
as leading only to despair
and separation. There's no need
that I can see for our affair
to necessarily proceed
to that far-off, depressing end.
I don't accept that fate is penned.'

8:39 pm

'I wish I shared your optimism,'
Rebecca counters. 'But I can't,
so let's engage in realism.
I'm not a naive débutante
as once I may have been; I'm cured
of that unhelpful self-delusion
that somehow seems to have endured
inside your head. Have no confusion
about this: happy ever after
does not exist. So don't expect it—
you'll end up hanging from a rafter
when finally you, too, reject it...
unless you do it now, before
it comes to haunt you evermore.'

8:42 pm

'How did you come to be so bitter?'
'Experience—you may have heard
of it.' 'You're acting like a quitter.
Reserve is just another word
for cowardice.' 'Sure, call me chicken—
whatever serves your ego better!
But don't expect your taunts to quicken
my extrication from the fetter
of common sense. That just won't work!
And neither will your reassurance
that no dread, prowling dangers lurk
behind each corner. My endurance
can stand against yours unabated:
so try me, and you'll be frustrated.'

8:45 pm

'I just might take you up on that,'
Glenn answers with determination.
'I may not be a diplomat
schooled in the science of oration,
but I've been known to talk all through
the night on an impassioned topic
like this—I've nothing else to do.'
'Well, I have. What are you, myopic
or something? Can't you see that I'm
already occupied tonight?
My partner here—in more than crime—
preceded you, so be polite
and give your arguments a miss.
Leave us alone. I'm sick of this.'

8:48 pm

Glenn looks at Fred; incomprehension
invades his stern-set features. He
had until now paid no attention
to Bec's companion, feeling free
to bare his soul to the presumed
exclusion of attentive ears.
Indignant as a disentombed
Egyptian mummy, he appears
to turn a shade of purple-blue
as he attempts—in vain—to quell
his anger. 'Who the hell are you?'
he fulminates: 'And why the hell
are you here with my girl?' 'I'm Fred...
and I suspect I've been misled.'

8:51 pm

'Well, not by me,' Rebecca pouts.
'I'm not his girl. I'm really not!'
'Well, this guy seems to have his doubts—'
Fred hesitates—'And I'm somewhat
confused as well.' 'It's simple, really,'
says Bec. 'We used to be an item;
we broke up—this is true, sincerely—
and he complains, ad infinitum,
because—for reasons of his own—
he's so reluctant to accept
the premise that we may have grown
apart that he's just overstepped
the boundary between reality
and unexplained irrationality.'

8:54 pm

'It looks as though you two have got
some sorting out to do,' says Fred.
'It seems, Bec, that your Lancelot
is somewhat sturdy in the head,
and you seem kind of stressed-out too.
It might be better if I left
you both alone.' Glenn says: 'Please do!
I don't appreciate your theft
of my beloved.' 'Calm down, mate.
I'm just an innocent bystander
in this; no reason you should hate
or hassle me. My role's Lysander
in this midsummer night's scenario—
an extra, not an impresario.'

8:57 pm

'Oh, Shakespeare? Not a bad allusion
considering it is, in fact,
the summer solstice.' Glenn's profusion
of sparring ways in which to act
leads him along this senseless tangent.
'If you're Lysander, who am I?'
'Let's see,' says Fred. 'You're stubborn, plangent
and loud... curriculum vitae
that would most certainly suggest
that Bottom is your perfect role!
Was that his name? Or have I messed
it up? It might be "Ass"—or "Hole",
for all I know! Bec, help me out.
You know the guy I'm on about.'

9:00 pm

'No, right first time,' corroborates
Rebecca. 'Bottom, noble weaver,
who, with his rustic acting mates
became a well-respected diva
of amateur production. But
You're Oberon, and not Lysander.
You drugged me when my eyes were shut,
encouraging me to philander
with this ass. I'm the fairy queen,
you see—Titania—and my mind,
though once deluded, is now keen,
my sense returned, and now I find
my vision straight, no longer wonky—
and I want you, and not this donkey.'

9:03 pm

Glenn's riled at this. 'I thought you said
that you were leaving,' he addresses
the tickled, madly-grinning Fred.
'I did say that...' the wit confesses.
'He's going nowhere,' Bec defends.
'He's staying here. You've got no right
to go and boss around my friends—
No, Fred! I need you here. Sit tight!'
'No, listen: on a sombre note,'
Fred says as he vacates his seat.
'I really think you should devote
some time to this. I won't compete
with Glenn here, so I'll call you later.'
He kisses Bec, who hisses: 'Traitor!'

9:06 pm

'You idiot!' Rebecca fumes
as Fred departs. 'What mental seizure
is this? What lunacy consumes
your mind, provoking such amnesia?
We've broken up, if you'll recall!
Since lunchtime, Glenn—or did I dream it?
You know, you've got a lot of gall.'
'I'm sorry—but I didn't deem it
a crime to try to win you back.'
Rebecca laughs, and says: 'Fat chance!
After your stupefying lack
of tact, you must be in a trance
if you expect me to return...
I think you've got a lot to learn.'

9:09 pm

'You know, you're making a mistake—'
'Oh, give up! I don't have to listen
to this—so go and bellyache
at someone else. Fred's right to christen
you Bottom: stubborn as a mule,
that's you! You've gone and wrecked my night,
subjected me to ridicule,
scared off my date—you neophyte!
You artless, bungling, stupid... *man!*
My God! You know, you're all the same!
You bully us—won't let us plan
our own lives—and expect acclaim
and gratitude for granting us
your slimy, patronising fuss!

9:12 pm

'It's more than any girl can stand,
who has a modicum of self
respect! I won't dance in your hand
like some submissive, bashful elf—
some Tinkerbell! Just go away.
I wanted you to be my friend—
I'm having second thoughts, to say
the least. What? Don't you comprehend
my subtle hinting? Read my lips!
Depart! Begone! Be over there!
Go buy a beer! Or eat some chips!
Seduce a woman! I don't care—
and let me be completely clear—
as long as you're no longer here.'

9:15 pm

Glenn's never known that words can stun
as if composed of concrete matter
until today. They weigh a tonne,
and hit him hard enough to splatter
his brain and heart and other organs
across the floor. Rebecca seems
to Glenn as vicious as a gorgons'
sorority; he almost screams
beneath the torture of his wound,
and, reeling, turns away, alone
like a poor castaway marooned
on some cold, frozen, arctic-zone
forgotten island of despair
and loneliness without compare.

9:18 pm

The sky has been discreetly fading
from deepened blue to empty black
for some time, leaving Kristin wading
through murky half-light, looking back
over her shoulder now and then,
cautiously forward and askance,
repeating ever and again
this nervous, wary, ritual dance
to ward off any poltergeist
or other spectral apparition
that might be on her heels, enticed
by twilight's dim, half-blind transition,
where shadows blur, and nightmares loom
against the rising, spreading gloom.

9:21 pm

The light is dead; the sound is muffled,
as if both world and time had stopped.
The air is still, the leaves unruffled,
and background silhouettes adopt
an aspect of unfocused haze,
their colours leached away, defined
in silent blacks and eerie greys.
Kris stumbles, clumsy as if blind,
straining to reconcile her eyes
between lost day and unborn night,
frustrated by the late demise
of colour and untroubled sight.
Her mind instructs her to be calm;
her body screams out in alarm.

9:24 pm

The dusk is vanishing, replaced
by inky blackness broken solely
by humming, flicking streetlights, spaced
at intervals like rows of holy
archangels sporting haloes glowing
with empty reassurance. High
above, a snatch of moon is showing
between the clouds, and by and by
is unveiled as a perfect whole,
pock-marked by darkened, ancient craters;
surrounded by an aureole
of luminescence. Navigators
have always looked aloft for aid:
Kris borrows from their ancient trade.

9:27 pm

Deciding that the moon's direction
is good as any, she endorses
this half-intuited election
by re-establishing her course's
alignment to this novel route.
She figures that if she proceeds
in one direction, resolute
and undeterred, she must of needs
stumble across some means of getting
back to the city. So assured
of leaving this unwelcome setting
behind—and more or less inured
to disappointment anyway—
she marches on without delay.

9:30 pm

Her confidence does not last long,
however. For it soon grows clear
that though her will and legs are strong,
she won't be able to adhere
to this regime of clueless striding
forever. As her body tires,
she feels her mental strength subsiding
until all trace of hope expires.
She stops and slumps against a post
beneath a pool of neon glare.
It's then she notices a host
of shadowed figures making their
suspicious way towards her spot—
she tenses in a panicked knot.

9:33 pm

In fear, she ducks into an alley
and waits for her potential foes
to pass. Eventually, they sally
beyond the buildings that enclose
her hiding place—their long, extended
shadows probe searchingly, and flicker
away—but one remains suspended
in mid-stride, while the others, quicker,
have passed him by. 'Hey, guys!' he hisses:
'There's something hiding here—come see!'
Kris shudders, thinking, 'Jesus—this is
the end... I'm dead!' She tries to flee
along the alley on discreet
tiptoes—but it's a dead-end street.

9:36 pm

The figures' looming silhouettes
obscure the alley's narrow shaft
as they creep forward. One upsets
a rubbish bin—a sudden draft
lifts crumpled paper on its breath
and sends it flapping down the lane—
he swears. The ancient shibboleth
imploring youngsters to abstain
from any dealing with a stranger—
brainwashed to *Brave New World* proportions—
fills Kristin's mind with sudden danger,
and grisly and grotesque distortions
of real life invade her thoughts
with gruesome, sinister reports.

9:39 pm

Unwashed and shabby, hair protruding
in all directions—held by dirt—
ill-fitting, crumpled clothes exuding
unpleasant odours, the overt
appearance of the shadowed group
that towers over Kristin's form
would unnerve any soldiers' troop,
let alone Kris, whose social norm—
of zero unemployment, pensions
and widespread social welfare greater
than any country—never mentions
that poverty's the procreator
of disadvantaged, homeless races
like the assembly she now faces.

9:42 pm

They seem to her as evil gnomes,
or grinning, diabolic trolls—
but, though they may be lacking homes,
they're not bereft of hearts or souls:
'Are you all right?' one asks sincerely.
'What are you doing, sitting here?'
Another says, 'She's frightened, clearly.'
And then to her: 'No need to fear.
I'm sure we'd never dream of hurting
a pretty girl like you!' 'Oh, Will,'
the third man cries. 'You're always flirting!
What must she think?' 'Well, you can grill
her if you want—but there's no vice
in simply trying to be nice!'

9:45 pm

'I'm not afraid of you,' Kris lies.
The men exchange triumphant glances.
'Listen! It talks!' their leader cries,
and with his arms outstretched advances
in what he hopes will be perceived
as friendliness: 'We come in peace!'
he says. Kris doesn't look relieved,
and shouts, 'I'll call for the police!
Stay back!' The figure looks quite hurt.
'Well, pardon me,' he says; his tone
and aspect serve to disconcert
her even further. 'You're alone,
and looked like you could use a hand—
does that deserve a reprimand?'

9:48 pm

Kris looks bewildered, but admits:
'Well, yeah, I'm kind of lost, I guess.'
'No shame in that,' he offers. 'It's
an obstacle I must confess
to falling foul of once or twice.
Where do you want to be?' 'A tram
or bus would certainly suffice—
if you could draw a diagram,
or give directions...' 'We'll do better!'
he offers. 'How about a train?'
'Direct me, and I'll be your debtor!
Thanks, really—' 'No, let me explain,'
she's interrupted. 'Come with us,
and find the railway station—thus!'

9:51 pm

Kris pauses, once again suspicious.
'No, it would be an imposition—'
'Come on, there's nothing surreptitious
about our moonlit expedition.
We're simply friends out for a stroll—
we mean no harm.' 'I'm sure you're nice—'
Kris does her utmost to console—
'But it would be against advice
to go with strangers.' 'Well, that's easy!'
he brightens. 'Let me introduce
myself! I'm Art. That's Ed. This sleazy,
if well-intentioned, poor excuse
for poetry is Will. And Zen
was here, but now she's gone again.'

9:54 pm

He claps his hands and gives a whistle,
and Zen comes bounding round the corner.
'I didn't offer your dismissal
to frolic with the local fauna,'
he castigates. 'No breaking ranks.'
Zen looks contrite, and takes her place
within the friendly, fond phalanx
that Kristin just can't quite embrace
as being actual and for real.
'I'm Kristin,' she admits, bemused
and less than sure she should reveal
that much. 'I'm sorry I accused
you all of being—you know—weird,
but that's the way you first appeared!'

9:57 pm

'Think nothing of it,' Arthur gestures
magnanimously. 'It's not rare
for people, seeing these old vestures,
these shabby shoes, this unwashed hair,
to think of us as somewhat shady.'
'But all the same, I didn't mean—'
'Apology accepted, lady,'
Art bows. 'I must admit, the scene
would look quite odd to an outsider.
But, seeing as we're all acquainted,
and ignorance—that great divider
of human beings—has been painted
out of existence: come! Let's gain
our passage on the nearest train.'

10:00 pm

Within a hundred metres, much
to the embarrassment of Kris,
they find the station. 'God, I'm such
a dope,' she says. 'How could I miss
the train-line at this paltry distance?'
'It's dark, I figure,' Art assuages.
'I'm glad that we could lend assistance—
you could have been out here for ages!'
They wait along the platform, lit
by lonely, dim, electric lamps,
until the signal lights emit
their warning. Kristin and the tramps
jump quickly to their feet, and wait
as clanging bells reverberate.

10:03 pm

The cheerful noise of booming bass
draws Zoe to the busy pub.
'At last,' she thinks. 'A lively place!
That lousy hotel supper club
might be my scene when I'm past forty,
but now, this better suits my taste.
Tonight I feel a trifle naughty,
and disinclined to being chaste.'
She feels adventure is in store—
perhaps the full moon hastens this—
and opportunities galore
come whispered in a static hiss
through stacks of pulsing, booming speakers
to wide and varied pleasure-seekers.

10:06 pm

Inside, Glenn sits against a wall,
absently watching people throwing
darts at their targets. Overall,
the image he succeeds in showing
is one of quietly detached
and unimposing catatonia,
as if his brain had been unlatched,
needing a good whiff of ammonia
to reinstate his conscious frame
of mind. A vacant, lifeless smile
appears as he attends the game,
his fascination infantile
but serving one important goal:
to wrap him tight and keep him whole.

10:09 pm

A badly-aimed projectile glances
against a wall, and is deflected
by the most unforeseen of chances
towards where Glenn sits, unprotected.
It misses him by molecules
and clatters on the floor. 'That's close!'
a man cries. 'Let me check the rules—
no points for scoring comatose
bystanders—try again!' 'That's right,'
Glenn murmurs. 'Take another shot.
Aim better this time, and you might
just hit me. No, go on—I've got
no better plans this evening than
a fun-filled amateur trepan.'

10:12 pm

'Hey, live a little,' one advises.
'And be a happy little camper.'
'Cheer up,' another sympathises.
'Be merry, and don't put a damper
on our night with your suicidal
soliloquies.' 'Don't get me wrong,'
Glenn warns. 'I'm not just spouting idle,
attention-seeking, overlong
and empty sentiments. Sincerely,
my life is meaningless.' 'Too bad,'
he's answered. 'Sleep it off; you've merely
had too much drink—it's known to add
to melancholy and depression!'
But cheery words make no impression.

10:15 pm

The players won't resume their match
until he's out of throwing distance—
apparently for fear he'll snatch
a dart, and with unbent persistence
make his quietus. And perhaps
he would—but not from bitter pain
or anguish; simply from his lapse
into a state of dull, mundane
existence, lacking any lustre.
He just feels empty, void of feeling,
without the faculty to muster
emotion; staring at the ceiling,
reflecting that its blank immensity
echoes his own subdued propensity.

10:18 pm

Protesting mildly, he arises
and makes a grand tour of the bar—
not a long trip, for it comprises
only two chambers, hardly far
apart, but resolutely blocked
by banks of human flesh that hinder
his progress. Jostled, pushed and knocked,
he feels a dully glowing cinder,
inflamed from somewhere deep inside
beneath a cold and dark exterior,
but capable—when over-tried—
of provocation to hysteria,
to conflagration quite divorced
from reason: torrid holocaust.

10:21 pm

Not wanting this to happen, he
heads quickly to the hotel's rear,
where he feels less constrained, more free;
where there exists an atmosphere
of cool night air that merits breathing.
The garden's open spaces heal
his consternation by bequeathing
to him an aspect of genteel
and almost tangible relief;
he pants hard in recuperation
and tries to comprehend the brief
excursion into desperation
that took him like a brain disease—
he drops his head between his knees.

10:24 pm

'That way lies madness,' he reflects,
not knowing that he's talked aloud
until a strange voice interjects
with clarity that pricks the shroud
of all-around narcotic stupor
enveloping his dampened senses.
'That way? Between your legs?' the snooper
proposes jestfully. Glenn tenses
and jerks his head up quickly. 'Oh,'
he says, in doubtful recognition.
'It's you. Hi.' His response is slow,
enfeebled by its sad position
beneath his mental carapace.
'So, did you find your special place?'

10:27 pm

'Depending on your definition,'
nods Zoe. 'On one hand, I've been
upon a fruitful expedition—
but on the other, I've not seen
anything like what I expected
to write about in terms of sights
for tourists. I've been misdirected,
I fear. No doubt this town invites
more scrutiny than I've applied,
but no immediate result
to my attempts to peer inside
has come to light—it's like a cult,
which I've no hope of penetrating;
I tell you, it's a bit frustrating.'

10:30 pm

Glenn's never ceased to be amazed
by some Americans' capacity
to talk about themselves, unfazed
at exercising their loquacity
on total strangers. Observations,
biographies, tall tales, opinions—
none are exempt from the narrations
of these communicative minions.
Whether besotted by their voices,
or truly anxious to impart
their wisdom, they allow few choices
of their disciples once they start
delivering their earnest speeches—
like prolix and tenacious leeches.

10:33 pm

'...And then this woman was afraid
I'd come to mug her,' Zo explains.
'When I attempted to persuade
the victim that I sought her brains
and not her purse, she wouldn't take
my word, but—' 'Gee, is that the time?'
Glenn interrupts: 'I'll never make
my bus at this rate! It's a crime
how early public transport dies
on weekends. Bye! I have to go!'
With this excuse, he turns and flies
convincingly away from Zo,
returning to the bar, where he
sits once more melancholily.

10:36 pm

Rebecca sees him there, and curses
beneath her breath. Why does he stay
when he's not wanted? What coerces
his will in such a stubborn way?
It's true, the often-quoted line
runs *If at first you don't succeed...*
but there are few so asinine
that their tenacious egos need
much more persuasion of their state
of undesirability than Bec's
delivered to her sometime mate.
His presence only serves to vex
her further, so she turns askance,
attempting to avoid his glance.

10:39 pm

Most of the hotel—Bec included—
is startled by a new arrival.
Presented plainly, face denuded
of make-up, clothes picked for survival
rather than glamour, stripped of jewels
and earrings, her austere appearance
could easily have kindled duels
and quests of peerless perseverance
in more romantic times. Men lust
and women envy as she saunters
towards the bar, but she's not fussed
by libertines or jealous taunters—
she's kept by modesty from knowing
the stir awakened by her showing.

10:42 pm

However, out of all the stares
provoked by the surprise debut
that Kristin's made this evening, there's
just one of recognition. Few
have yet enjoyed the opportunity
to meet this wanderer, since she's
a transient in the community,
having arrived from overseas
so recently. Rebecca knows
her face, though, from this morning's meeting—
if furtive glances might compose
acquaintance, when exchanged in fleeting,
ephemeral and brief succession—
a moment's bookshop indiscretion.

10:45 pm

Kristin appears to partly share
her recollection, for she stands
and stares back, as if asking where,
in all the widely-scattered lands
she's travelled, have they met before?
She frowns, and struggles to locate
this face in memory, to draw
a context, circumstance or date
that might address the deja vu
surrounding this half-solved enigma.
'This drives me crazy—who are you?'
she grins, remembering the stigma
attached to ignorance like this:
'Sorry for asking—here, I'm Kris.'

10:48 pm

'And I'm Rebecca,' says the latter:
'You came into my shop—' 'That's right!
I plain forgot.' 'It doesn't matter.
I'm glad that you weren't too polite
to ask!' 'Well, that's one thing I'm not;
no need to worry.' '*Kris*,' Bec muses
over the name: 'That's short for—what?
Christina? Crystal?' 'Please!' effuses
the so-called: 'Nothing quite so silly.
It's short for Kristin.' 'Kristin—where's
that from?' 'From Denmark: home of chilly
conditions, well-paved thoroughfares,
of Hamlet, Lego, Carlsberg, ski
resorts, of pastry—and of me!'

10:51 pm

She grins again—again, Bec sees
deep in her eyes a subtle flicker,
lasting just long enough to seize
attention, disappearing quicker
than thought: a brief, uncertain shift,
an indiscernible exchange,
a flash too fleeting and too swift
to fall within the clumsy range
of comprehension. Nonetheless,
what eyes may doubt, and mind dismiss,
remains for feeling to assess—
and Bec, when pondering on Kris,
feels feelings come from all directions
in new and unconceived collections.

10:54 pm

Perhaps it's just the way Kris gazes
directly, deep into the eyes
of those she talks to that amazes
Rebecca. Or, to analyse
a little further, maybe it's
the way she seems to fill all space
available—the way she sits
at ease, as if she owned the place,
the way her body seems connected
directly to a mind controlling
its subject perfectly, projected
expansively in seamless, rolling
and smoothly-executed action,
brimming with easy satisfaction.

10:57 pm

No matter what the reason, though,
Rebecca finds herself entranced,
enchanted by the inner glow
of this strange traveller she's chanced
to meet from half a world away.
With wonder she becomes aware
that truant thoughts no longer stray
to Glenn, or her collapsed affair,
or any subject: all seem trivial,
hopelessly distant when contrasted
with this delightfully convivial
exchange. If she's a little plastered,
that just serves to enhance the state
that Kristin's many charms create.

11:00 pm

'This place is crowded,' she confides.
'Let's go; I'll take you on a tour
of town to rival any guide's
mostly-invented overture.'
'You've got a deal,' says Kristin, flashing
another exercise in charm.
A second later, they're both crashing
towards the doorway, arm in arm,
jostling for passage, and emerging
inevitably on the street,
where straggling queues are still converging
from every compass point to meet
a poorer pub no longer blessed
by Bec and unexpected guest.

11:03 pm

Glenn looks up from the bar to see
that Bec's no longer where she sat.
Discreetly as an escapee
she's vanished without caveat,
leaving her place unoccupied—
a vacuum in a world of flesh—
until the crushing bodies hide
her haven with their seething mesh
of life. Glenn looks around him, frantic,
searching the pub from wall to wall,
and spots Bec and her transatlantic
companion—but he doesn't call,
for they're outside and walking yonder,
while Glenn is left to sit and ponder.

11:06 pm

At first he can't believe she'd just
leave him like that. He waits a second,
secure in the decreasing trust
that she'll return soon, having reckoned
she'd give him something of a shock
in playful, jocular good-humour.
The onward marching of the clock
convinces him this self-told rumour
is somewhat ludicrous, however.
What would she prove, or learn, or gain
from such a juvenile endeavour?
Insistently, a sad refrain
repeats until it's understood
inside his head: *she's gone for good.*

11:09 pm

He stands up slowly, half-resigned
to what he is about to do.
He knows he has to rid his mind
of the unwanted residue
of memory and painful thought;
he must immerse and drown his sorrow—
though not in toxic spirits, bought
tonight, regretted all tomorrow,
but in an anaesthetic much
more powerful, and more addictive:
in sympathy and tender touch,
in passion frank and unrestrictive—
possibly bitter, self-deceiving
and callous, but no less relieving.

11:12 pm

Returning once again outside,
he sees that Zoe's still reclining
beneath a tree. 'I've got no ride;
I missed the bus, so I'm resigning
myself to staying here until
I find a taxi or a friend—
or morning comes,' he says. 'You're still
around—I'm glad!' 'Since I can spend
my time and money as I please,'
Zo answers, 'I don't see why not.
Carpe diem, they tell us: *seize*
the day. Or night. I don't care what
you seize, exactly, come to think!
Whatever. How about a drink?'

11:15 pm

'Sounds good to me,' Glenn says, and swallows
the nervous lump inside his throat.
Zo ploughs towards the bar; he follows,
not knowing this routine by rote—
having no clue—but improvising
as best he can. He's somewhat rusty
and quite unused to fraternising
with this intention, but his trusty
spontaneous initiative
informs his wandering ad-lib,
combining with his wit to give
his speech an air of easy, glib,
self-confident, well-practised sparkle,
hedging against his feared debacle.

11:18 pm

Though not unhandsome, through his youth
Glenn couldn't be accused of leading
a life of lechery: no sleuth,
however resolute his pleading,
could hope to truthfully uncover
much evidence of promiscuity
if paid to do so—no true lover
before Rebecca, an annuity
of sad and empty letterboxes
marking each day of Valentine
in years gone by. No equinoxes
or solstices changed this design—
through plodding days and stretching seasons,
he stayed alone, for untold reasons.

11:21 pm

And so, he finds this situation
a little daunting. What to say?
What irresistible temptation
to offer? His naiveté
bewilders him, and makes a battle
of what has always seemed so smooth
in movies, where seducers rattle
suave strings of sentiment to soothe
even the most impeding qualms.
It's all that Glenn can do to keep
abreast of his half-stuttered charms,
hoping he doesn't sound a creep
but fearing this to be the case
in this odd, self-pursuing chase.

11:24 pm

Of course, he needn't worry so.
For Zoe, with compunction lifted
somewhat by alcohol, has no
criterion of smooth and gifted
loquacity Glenn should concern
himself with meeting. Words are wasted,
superfluous, where taciturn
assent, however briefly tasted,
is ultimately all required
by strangers striving to unite
their lonely selves with their desired
companions. It's a pre-won fight,
towards a termination guided
by causal factors long decided.

11:27 pm

The repartee and quick rapport,
the thinly-veiled insinuation,
the tales received in tones of awe
of past achievement, the inflation
of egos, words that praise and flatter—
all these are scenery, the icing
upon the cake. They just don't matter.
They're obsolete; their sacrificing
would make no odds, save saving time.
The two are reservoirs of pure
submission, but the paradigm
of carefully-concealed allure
keeps them apart, engaged in song
and tactful dance—if not for long.

11:30 pm

'What'll it be?' Zo shouts, competing
against the noise. Glenn doesn't hear,
and cries, 'I'm sorry?' Zo, repeating
her question louder in his ear,
casually takes him by the shoulder;
they ripple at the touch. Glenn answers,
feeling more fortified, and bolder,
seizing her slender waist. Like dancers
caught in a still, unmoving waltz,
they stand, combined, while their exchange
is made. When finished, though their false
excuse for keeping up this strange
position may no longer bear,
it's clear that neither of them care.

11:33 pm

United by a common fear
of solitude—of separation—
and both prepared to persevere
to any lengths for their salvation
from loneliness tonight, they grow
forever closer as they stand
amid the tavern's ebb and flow,
protected by a tightening band
impermeable to intrusion
and banishing to distant reaches
all scruples or concerns. Their fusion
into a single soul impeaches
the despot of the world outside;
that tyrant wrongly deified.

11:36 pm

'You said you had no way of getting
back home,' says Zoe: 'Buses, trains
have stopped, and there's no way I'm letting
you pay a taxi fare.' Glenn feigns
distress: 'I guess that means I'm staying
awake till morning, then—or sleeping
rough on the street.' 'I wasn't saying
you should do that! I won't be keeping
you out all night—I only thought
that since I've got a hotel suite
just blocks away—well, any port
when in a storm, you know...' 'Repeat
that one more time?' is Glenn's request:
'You're asking me to be your guest?'

11:39 pm

'I guess so, yeah,' Zo answers, smiling
with faint embarrassment: 'I mean,
it's a nice place: the view's beguiling,
the mini-bar is full. Between
the sofa and the king-size bed—'
She blushes here—'I'm sure we'll find
a place for you to rest your head.'
Glenn smiles: 'I've never yet declined
such an appealing offer from
someone so tantalising!' Rushes
of angry mental conflicts bomb
his conscience, but he briskly brushes
them all aside: 'I can't say no.
Thanks for your charity—let's go.'

11:42 pm

Outside, the streets are still and bare,
with hurried groups of people scattered
irregularly here and there,
the lingering, divided, tattered
remains of daytime crowds. The mall
provides a makeshift auditorium
for late-night buskers, who install
themselves in doorways in memoriam
of sunlight's lively bustle, flaunting
their passionate and rough-edged muse
to all the passing spirits haunting
the pavement still. Their sounds suffuse
along the silent thoroughfare,
and echo, lonely, through the air.

11:45 pm

'It's all so quiet,' Kris declares,
'As if the world had gone to sleep.'
'It has,' explains Rebecca. 'There's
not much to do at night but creep
stealthily round the streets like this,
as if perpetually afraid
of waking someone up—I'd miss
the far more scintillating shade
of nightlife in Berlin—New York—
if I were you.' 'They're great, it's true,
but still, I'd sometimes rather talk
than party—meeting someone new
is one of travelling's great joys,
far more than flashing lights and noise.

11:48 pm

'To see you all about your lives,
so alien and different, yet
so much in common—that's what drives
me ever onward. Rome, Tibet
or Timbuktu—no matter where
you go, no matter what you do,
it's fascinating to compare
experiences you accrue
as you go on. Each new encounter
is wonderful and special, whether
you sit beneath a tree, or mount a
risky descent into the nether
extremities of some great valley—
or hear a busker in an alley.'

11:51 pm

'I know which option I'd prefer,'
Rebecca says. Kris answers, 'Well,
to meet a willing raconteur—
a foreigner with tales to tell—
to me is always more inspiring.
For only people are unique,
forever novel, never tiring,
possessed of intrigue and mystique—
and unpredictable, to boot.'
Rebecca smiles: 'I'll do my best
to live up to this attribute
of mystery you seem to vest
in folks like us—can I fulfil
your hopes?' Kris beams: 'I'm sure you will.'

11:54 pm

They come across a stony wall,
skulking beneath a mass of trees
that tower, sentinel and tall,
and flaunt botanic pedigrees
at anyone who travels past
their terrace. 'What's in there?' asks Kris.
'What secret—unimagined, vast—
do these cold, sombre walls dismiss?'
'In there?' Rebecca says. 'Botanic
gardens: a lake, shrubs, trees, some flowers,
a duck or two—and black Satanic
processions in the smallest hours
of full-moon nights, if you believe
the stories schoolchildren conceive.'

11:57 pm

'That sounds exciting,' Kris enthuses.
'Tonight's a full moon—not to mention
also a solstice.' She peruses
with somewhat dubious intention
the heavy gate, securely laden
with chains and padlocks, that frustrates
their entrance. 'God—an iron maiden
sunk in a moat with leaden weights
and welded shut could hardly be
impregnable as this,' Kris sighs:
'A pity—I'd quite like to see
the inside. Would it be unwise,
do you suppose, to scale the fence?'
'No,' says Rebecca. 'That makes sense.'

12:00 am

They wait until the coast is clear—
not long; the traffic's been reduced
to lonely stragglers chancing near
infrequently. Bec gives a boost
to Kristin, launching her atop
the wall, and scrambles up behind.
Pausing, they contemplate the drop
before them—shadows, ill-defined
along the wall like tightrope-walkers—
then plunge headlong through darkness, falling
and rolling on the ground as stalkers
occupied in some heist, then crawling
arm over arm as blackness folds
across its ominous thresholds.

12:03 am

They rise a second later, brushing
loose flecks of dirt and sticks of bark
from skin and clothes. The silence, hushing
even their breathing in the dark
eternity, impresses both:
they stand unnerved within a jungle
of wiry, tangled undergrowth,
upon a carpet lush with fungal
abundance—till their startled eyes
become accustomed to the lack
of light, and they can analyse
the formless, many-fingered, black
(malevolent?) and sprawling shapes
that clothe the world in tattered drapes.

12:06 am

It's like another planet: bathed
in eerie moonlight, kept apart
from all the outer world, unscathed
by steel and stone, within the heart
of metropolitan surrounds.
Dim, fragile lights, like fairy torches
are set throughout the sprawling grounds;
the starlight soothes but never scorches.
They walk past dormant flowerbeds,
where foxgloves, snowdrops, hyacinths
and lilies rest their weary heads;
through verdant mazes, labyrinths
of hedgerow, thicket, glade and clearing—
a prize of nature's engineering.

12:09 am

They stroll beside a lake, expecting
a frog to break its jet-black water
with golden ball in hand, collecting
the same for some king's virgin daughter.
They search the ground for leprechauns,
and notice now and then a glint
of light reflected from the horns
of elfin folk—but as they squint
against the darkness, fauns and satyrs
go scurrying in all directions
to tend to unknown fairy matters,
removed from sight. The lake's reflections
hold unsure glimpses, brief and fleeting—
no conversation, only greeting.

12:12 am

'My boyfriend used to bring me here,'
Rebecca reminisces. 'He'd
sit down with me, and persevere
in vain to demonstrate the need
for complex numbers, differentials
and integrals, surds, matrices
and mathematical essentials
of all descriptions such as these.
He studied maths, you see—but still
appreciated things of beauty:
an artist of no little skill,
I always knew.' 'He sounds a cutie,'
says Kris, half-joking, but half-serious.
'He was—but sadly deleterious.'

12:15 am

Kris lifts her eyebrows. 'Oh? Do tell.'
Bec shrugs: 'Not much to tell. He got
a little close, is all. From swell
to sweltering, you know: somewhat
distressing for a modern girl
who likes her liberty.' 'You're right,'
says Kristin. 'How can you unfurl
your wings, and fly as if as light
as air, when there's the leaden weight
of manacles around your heels,
disguised as lover, partner, mate?
Such dank imprisonment appeals
only to those too insecure
to disregard their freedom's lure.'

12:18 am

'Your sentiments are quite severe,'
Rebecca says. 'But nonetheless
they hold a lot of truth, I fear.'
Kris ponders this, and answers, 'Yes.'
Their footsteps, crunching on the gravel,
provide the only barricade
against the silence as they travel
along the path like renegade
taxonomists comparing plants
illicitly beneath the cloak
of darkness. Tender air enchants
their spirits, and the stars provoke
a sense of magic so complete
that life's conundrums can't compete.

12:21 am

It's in this cool, untroubled state
That they first notice that the path
is glowing fiercely—like a great
debris of cinders in a hearth—
as if the road were paved with gold.
Their shadows loom before them, leaping
and flickering in uncontrolled
delirium, like demons sweeping
across the night. They whirl around
to meet a pair of fiery eyes
approaching with a crunching sound.
Predicting imminent demise
they flee this sudden source of danger:
this truck—and inside, this park ranger.

12:24 am

The wheels spin in reverse gear, spewing
a spray of pebbles as the ute
backs up. 'Whatever are we doing?
If we get caught, he'll prosecute—'
Kris gasps as they attempt evasion—
'I'll go to jail, or be deported—'
'No need to offer me persuasion,'
Rebecca pants. 'Our plan's aborted—
if we escape with both our lives,
I'll be amazed.' They dart and pelt
still faster as the ranger drives
behind—a poacher on the veldt,
pursuing fleet, defenceless game
to catch, domesticate, and tame.

12:27 am

They leave the path for trees; reversing,
the car skids roughly to a halt.
The driver takes a torch and, cursing
as if considering assault,
continues his pursuit on foot.
His quarries, crashing madly through
assorted trees and bushes, put
a dozen metres—maybe two—
between themselves and their pursuer,
but he continues with conviction,
determined that no evildoer
will err within his jurisdiction
without the corresponding penance—
he owes this to his floral tenants.

12:30 am

They duck into a courtyard, hiding
behind a sombre concrete bust
within an alcove—not providing
much cover, but enough to trust
in such a manifest emergency.
The ranger rounds a corner, sweeping
his torch along the walls; their urgency
increases as the light comes creeping
towards their den. They close their eyes
and huddle in the corner, shrinking
small as they can, but this disguise—
despite their fervent wishful thinking—
does little to deter their foe
or dull his searchlight's probing glow.

12:33 am

They feel the light upon them—warm,
it almost seems, accusing, gloating—
dancing across each crouching form
in taunting victory, denoting
its conquest and their base betrayal.
Kris whispers, 'No! *Nil desperandum!*
We've come this far—we can't now fail!'
She leaps and runs off in a random
direction, which Bec feels compelled
to follow. 'Now I've got you!' shouts
the ranger. 'Vandals! Punks! You've held
your final rampage hereabouts!
You won't kill one more bush, or vine,
or fern, or evergreen: you're mine!'

12:36 am

But Kris and Bec evade his grasp,
ducking beneath his flailing arms
and leaving him behind to gasp
in rage as they escape from harm's
frustrated reaches. Their reprieve
is necessarily too brief,
however: they can't hope to leave
the ranger stupefied with grief
after this temporary failure—
he's much more obstinate than that:
he'd follow them around Australia,
a vigilante bureaucrat;
his rage and his resolve would harden
until he had avenged his garden.

12:39 am

And so, the chase continues. Past
perennials and eucalypts,
through hillocks delicately grassed,
down arbours grown in leafy crypts,
around the lake, between the rocks—
it all becomes a bit surreal,
as if, by Xeno's paradox,
they're doomed to suffer this ordeal
indefinitely, and the ranger
will chase, but never catch, for all
eternity. It's even stranger
that none of their attempts to stall
among the mangrove or mimosa
succeed—he just grows ever closer.

12:42 am

'What is this guy, a cybernetic
automaton in human form
sent to pursue us with prosthetic,
untiring limbs?' They dodge a swarm
of swirling insects. 'Quick, we've got
to lose him—I can't last much longer!'
pants Kris, declining to a trot
as gradually the ranger's stronger,
inhuman paces bring him nearer.
'We're done for!' Bec despairs. 'This spells
the termination of an era
of freedom!' 'Maybe not!' Kris yells,
and sends Rebecca through a bush
with one effective, well-aimed push.

12:45 am

As Bec is lost from sight behind
the undergrowth, the ranger rounds
the bend, and is about to find
Kris standing there when she confounds
discovery by quickly diving
across the brake to follow Bec
to safety—soaring high, arriving
clumsily in a tangled wreck
on top of her companion. Lying
full-length upon Rebecca, hand
across her mouth to stop her trying
to speak or move, Kris hadn't planned
for it to happen quite this way—
but if it works, then it can stay.

12:48 am

Rebecca stares with curiosity,
and Kristin answers with a frown,
afraid additional verbosity
will bring the ranger's vengeance down
upon them. They can hear him searching
among the bushes, which they fear
will separate to show him lurching
towards them, should he overhear
the faintest cracking of a stick
or rustling of a leaf. Their hearts
are palpitating loud and quick
enough to hear—but he departs
oblivious, his footsteps fading
against the silence now invading.

12:51 am

Catastrophe averted, Kris
relaxes—but does not displace—
her hold on Bec. 'Good going, sis,'
she says. Restraint becomes embrace
as they exhale, congratulate
each other on their glad escape
and seriously contemplate
the gravity of this near scrape—
then, suddenly, break into grins
and simultaneously burst
out giggling like hysteric twins,
enclosed in fellowship, immersed
in undergrowth and friendship's hold,
shrieking with laughter uncontrolled.

12:54 am

Their hold grows tighter as they lie
in this improbable position
beneath the trees and starry sky.
With the eventual attrition
of their interminable bouts
of nervous laughter comes a new
emotion, bringing with it doubts
and vague uncertainties, but too
insistent for offhand denial.
A steady gaze unites their eyes
in searching, intimate espial;
they share one soul; they empathise
completely in all-knowing bliss;
they know each other's thoughts. They kiss.

12:57 am

A thousand thoughts go racing through
Rebecca's mind, but she's unable
in this confusion to construe
much meaning from their vast, unstable
invasion. Only her arousal
is constant: torrents of objections
and worries resolutely tousle
her will in opposite directions,
but these are fleeting, ineffectual;
such an experience of passion
can't be defused by intellectual
appeals to taste, taboo and fashion.
Her instinct leads her to intuit
as follows: if it feels good, do it.

1:00 am

And so, instead of holding back,
she lets her essence be consumed
by this impetuous attack
of feeling. Kristin's skin—perfumed
as hers is by a fragrant sheen
of perspiration—glistens, soft
and sumptuous as velveteen:
no man who ever held aloft
a razor blade could hope to boast
a face so sensuous to touch
as this. Their contact brings a host
of tactile excitations such
as these; their bodies melt together,
supple as willow, light as feather.

1:03 am

Their clothes are cast aside—a nuisance
dispensed with gladly—and their skins,
aglow with opaline translucence,
are all they wear apart from grins.
They let their hands roam free, exploring
each others' warmly-trembling curves,
as if engaged in contest, warring
to stimulate the others' nerves
to almost-painfully delicious
extremes. Their hearts pound faster, furious,
as they approach with avaricious
acceleration the luxurious
explosion—terrifying, thrilling—
of climax, flawlessly fulfilling.

1:06 am

The hotel lights are dimmed; *Bolero*
spins on Zo's portable CD
machine; the blinds are drawn. No pharoah
upon his throne could hope to see
such a delectable collection
of strawberries and cream, champagne
and caviar; a small selection
of empty bottles helps explain
the laid-back, easy-going aura
that bathes the room. The Latin score
sees one American señora
spinning her unprepared señor
across the room in three-four time,
despite their foreign, southern clime.

1:09 am

'I'm sorry, I've got two left feet,'
says Glenn. 'Well, maybe three or four,
to be more honest.' 'No! You're fleet
as any mountain goat—or more!'
protests his partner as they stumble
across a sofa and go crashing
towards the ground. 'At least you're humble,
at any rate,' she offers, smashing
her head against a table. 'Ouch.'
'Enough of dancing, anyway,'
says Glenn, reclining on the couch
invitingly. 'Why don't we play
a different game—it's lots of fun—
for adults only—know the one?'

1:12 am

'Assuming you don't mean canasta,'
Zo says, 'I think I get your drift.'
Glenn grins: 'You're smart as Zoroaster,
and cuter too.' 'Shut up, and shift
across so I can sit by you,'
she urges. Glenn moves duly over,
hardly impatient to eschew
her company. As bossa nova
comes flooding through the room, the moon
shines resolutely through a curtain.
The stage is set and dressed, and soon—
it's more than reasonably certain—
first lights and camera, and then action
will burst from this withheld attraction.

1:15 am

'I can't believe that I'm still necking
on sofas, like an adolescent
tormented by her parents' checking
up on her stolen, evanescent
experiments in timid sex,'
says Zoe as she frees her lips
from their first kiss. 'Even these treks
and convoluted worldwide trips
don't comfort me; I'm still concerned
that they'll come storming from New York,
having mysteriously learned
that I'm engaged in more than talk
with some Australian freshly picked
from off the streets!—They're rather strict.'

1:18 am

'At least you have some,' Glenn laments.
'Although they're far away, you know
that if your life gets too intense
they'll be there. Me, I had to grow
up all alone, and it was rough.'
'Poor baby,' Zoe murmurs, kissing
his ear. 'I guess it's made you tough—
and you don't know what you've been missing
in terms of argument and stress!
I've wished my parents to their graves
more times than once, I must confess—
but no more bad thoughts.' Zoe waves
her hand genteelly in the air
and keeps his spirits from despair.

1:21 am

Their touch is gentle, languid, patient,
as if delivered in slow motion.
Diminished by the stupefacient
surrounds, their previous commotion
yields to a hesitant approach,
incapable of being rushed.
Their bodies, faces, limbs encroach
inevitably, slowly, flushed
and feverish despite their halting
advance—the flame burns still and calm
without disturbing or assaulting,
providing warmth instead of harm;
but no less fervent is the heat
that its unhurried flares secrete.

1:24 am

Some fourteen floors below, the lobby
adjoins an opulent casino,
where folks pursue an ancient hobby
common to Monte Carlo, Reno
and Vegas. Dressed in gowns, tuxedos
and charm, the cream of high society
maintain aristocratic credos,
avoiding any impropriety
as they punctiliously mingle
between the blackjack and roulette,
amid the ever-present jingle
of coins and chips—to drink, to bet
exorbitant amounts of cash
that won't be missed: to show panache.

1:27 am

A group moves raggedly across
the foyer, laughing, slapping backs,
exhibiting a polished gloss
as smooth and shining as the wax
that coats the floor. Rock hides among
their numbers, artfully enclosed:
hanging upon this lowest rung
of social ladders, unopposed
by any doorman's interjection,
he bursts upon the armoured keep,
using these strangers for protection
like Ulysses employing sheep
to exit from the Cyclops' cave—
though Rock's another kind of slave.

1:30 am

Inside, he looks around in awe,
disoriented as a thief
who's stolen through an unwatched door
of paradise. With disbelief
he notices his face reflected
a thousand times in mirrored glass,
distorted out of shape, projected
on surfaces of polished brass.
The splendour takes him by surprise;
he can't do more than mutely gaze
in wonder at the scene that lies
before him: tables green with baize,
pillars of marble decked with gold—
a lustrous image to behold.

1:33 am

He apprehends an unknown feeling
as he observes these people betting,
conversing, drinking, spinning, dealing,
alluring, tantalising, whetting
his appetite—his ardent yearning
for understanding. What he senses
is like the unannounced returning
of some past life's experiences,
and he can't shake the deja vu
that haunts his disconcerted mind
until he's able to construe
the nature of this unaligned
effect... He doesn't have to comb
for long—it's this: he feels at home.

1:36 am

At home—at last! No more removed
from what he's always deeply felt
to be his station, he's improved
upon the hand that fate has dealt
(he always knew the deck was stacked)
and finds himself among a caste
of peers who all appear to act
and think the same as him. At last!
Companions he can emulate
instead of guiltily evading—
with whom he can associate
until his memories—degrading,
painful to think upon—are veiled
in good times, welcomed and regaled.

1:39 am

He wastes no time, and soon approaches
a lady decked in flowing finery—
shining with necklaces and brooches,
and smelling like a high-class winery:
'Excuse me, ma'am,' he says. 'I've spent
so much tonight—with such bad luck—
that I'm down to my bottom cent,
and now I find that I'm quite stuck
for cash. I wonder—could I borrow
a little? I can guarantee
I'll pay it back, in full, tomorrow.
Sir Weathernose will vouch for me—
you know him? No? Lord Wilberforce?
Dame Frupp? I've met them all, of course.'

1:42 am

The woman glances up and down
at Rock's incongruous appearance:
'I didn't know we had a clown
tonight,' she says. 'Your incoherence
is rather charming, little man.
Can you do any magic tricks?'
He's stunned: 'I'm not a courtesan
commissioned to provide your fix
of entertainment!' he explodes.
'Are you so blind that you can't see
that we're not ruled by different codes—
we're just the same!' She laughs in glee:
'I'm sorry if I sounded spiteful,
dear clown. Your humour's quite delightful!'

1:45 am

With this, she turns and walks away,
oblivious to Rocky's pleading.
'A victim of descent's decay,'
he postulates. 'I blame inbreeding.
She's evidently mad—completely!'
But subsequent attempts turn out
the same, no matter how discreetly
and slyly he proceeds to scout
the hall for a potential donor.
They turn away and cut him dead,
informing him that he's persona
non grata, parvenu, ill-bred,
and turning up collective noses
at any offer he proposes.

1:48 am

He stutters, 'No, but—', 'Please—' and 'What—'
as stone-faced masses pass him by.
They leave him rooted to the spot,
his hand outstretched to signify
the tragedy of his demotion
from nobleman to parasite.
These targets of lifelong devotion—
these upper classes—shine a light
on what he's spent so long denying.
His self-deluding bubble's burst;
he exits briskly, stumbling, crying,
filled with an all-consuming thirst
to join with this exalted clan,
but knowing that he never can.

1:51 am

The river taciturnly flows
jet-black between its grassy banks,
a patient study in repose,
delivering its untold tanks
of water between distant weirs,
pouring its dark and silent masses
so languidly that it appears
to be composed of black molasses,
oozing by trees and concrete bridges,
by walking tracks and rowing sheds,
breeding mosquitoes, gnats and midges
deep in its muddy, silted beds,
reflecting brief illuminations
of moonlight on its undulations.

1:54 am

A shadowed figure slowly shuffles
along the waterfront. The grass
beneath his shoeless footsteps muffles
the sound of his existence; sparse,
inscrutable enunciations
are all he makes by way of noise—
half-formed, despairing exclamations
suggesting that he knows no joys,
no comforts. Now he halts beside
the river, reaches in his coat
and hurls a shining object wide
out from the bank. It doesn't float
but sinks beneath the silent water
as if it were encased in mortar.

1:57 am

'Excuse me—littering's illegal
around here!' Arthur shouts, emerging
from darkness. 'So however regal
your lordship might be, don't go purging
your rubbish in this hapless river—
it isn't pious to pollute.
What was that poor, discarded sliver
of silver, anyway?' 'My flute,'
says Rocky, sounding quite dejected.
'I'm ditching it. It didn't work
in quite the manner I'd expected;
it's better suited to the murk
and mud than to society—
in that way, it's a bit like me.'

2:00 am

'Well, join the club!' says Arthur, grinning.
'Join me, and Ed, and Will, and Zen.
It's true, we've got no hope of winning
a Nobel Prize for style, but when
did we let that get us depressed?
It's like I said this morning: lives
like ours must rate among the best
in all the world. Where freedom thrives,
what more is needed? There's a place
for you among us always, Rock.
Providing you can take the pace
without too great a culture shock,
I promise you, we'll live like gods.
What do you say?' Rock simply nods.

2:03 am

Above them, quite a steamy scene
is taking place in Zoe's room.
As if composed of plasticine,
she and her temporary groom
lie intertwined in strained contortions
across her bed. Her lingerie
reveals her sensuous proportions,
and he wears boxer shorts. They sway
and ripple, moulded by the force
of passion, kissing, touching, holding,
hearts palpitating, voices hoarse,
hair tousled, limbs and bodies folding
upon each other like a puzzle
as they proceed to neck and nuzzle.

2:06 am

And suddenly their clothes are gone
and Zoe's pale and naked form
confronts him, stretching like a swan—
enchanting, graceful, white, soft, warm,
her body curves away before
his almost-disbelieving eyes.
He steps back, trying to restore
his nerve, as she proceeds to rise
and stands before him, tightly wrapping
her slender arms around his torso.
He feels their bodies overlapping
as they were once, but now are more so—
connected in a thousand places,
from arms, legs, stomachs, chests, to faces.

2:09 am

They press against each other, feeling
the sweat upon their bodies run
together, like a lotion healing
their bruises, aches and pains till none
remain to ail them—whether inner
or outer, physical or mental—
rubbing their skins forever thinner
until their bodies flow with gentle
determination through their weak
delineations and are mixed—
an indivisible physique
located in the space betwixt
their bodies, which no longer seem
as much incarnate flesh as dream.

2:12 am

He runs his fingers through her shock
of flowing, fiery, orange hair,
entwining each flame-coloured lock
around his fingers in a flare
of copper, kissing every inch
of flesh exposed above her waist—
then, noticing she doesn't flinch
at this, he moves to parts less chaste.
She bends beneath his roving touch,
accommodating and resisting
by turns, and tightening her clutch
around him, writhing, gasping, twisting
her body ever to and fro
and quivering from head to toe.

2:15 am

She leans once more upon the bed,
and pulls him gently after till
he lies, with arms and legs outspread,
above her body, poised to fill
her so completely with his essence
she knows her soul will overflow
in surging, bursting effervescence.
He halts atop this high plateau,
and looks so deeply in her eyes
with such a long, fixated stare
that they appear to hypnotise
him fully with their jade-green glare—
she's only seen such an impasse
reflected in a looking-glass.

2:18 am

Glenn gazes at these orbs of green,
and everything around them fades
to background—for he's only seen
such luminous and dancing shades
within one other person's face.
Their circles fill his field of vision,
free-floating, motionless, in space,
and match with absolute precision
the eyes that haunt his mind forever—
the image branded in his skull,
the knot he couldn't hope to sever,
the marriage that he can't annul—
it takes no time to recognise
he's staring at Rebecca's eyes.

2:21 am

And, focused on this common point,
his partner's body seems to melt
and resolidify—each joint
and curve of flesh along her svelte
and supple figure subtly shifts
into a more familiar form
as Glenn's imagination drifts
tangentially—as is the norm—
and he's no longer kissing Zoe
but someone else whose hair is black
instead of red, her skin not snowy
but tanned to gold; who leads him back
cavorting gladly through the past,
despite ostensible contrast.

2:24 am

'I missed you, babe,' he tells the eyes—
but suddenly he sees a fleck
where none belongs, and their disguise
is rendered void. 'But—you're not Bec,'
he almost utters. And he's right:
for here's a flaw he doesn't know,
and there, her eyes reflect the light
in quite a different way, and Zo
shows nuances and strange expressions
quite alien to Becca's gleams.
He can no longer make concessions
or compromises to his dreams—
it's useless, now, to keep defending
the fantasy he's been pretending.

2:27 am

He takes a final look, and sees
that even Zoe's shade of green
is foreign to his expertise.
Some differentiated gene—
some single strand of DNA—
has altered it the merest fraction.
The uninformed could never say
that this was so, but Glenn's reaction,
that of a practised connoisseur,
is more discerning—he could spot
the rogue genetic saboteur
a mile away—and like a shot
he knows that this will never work.
'My God,' he says. 'I've been a jerk.'

2:30 am

'Excuse me—what?' says Zoe, roused.
'Don't stop—it's time to make a purchase,
considering the time we've browsed!
No one's about to stop and search us;
we're all alone, the night is fine—
no, more than that: it's perfect. Look!
The moon is full. The stars, the wine:
it's like the chapter of a book,
or movie shot in steamy focus.
It's magic, Glenn—I know you feel it!
Abracadabra! Hocus-pocus!
Your soul is soaring—don't conceal it;
we can't retreat from this attack—
don't walk away from me—come back!'

2:33 am

Glenn stands against the corner, fuming.
His head is bowed; his back is turned.
He's burning with an all-consuming
frustration over what he's learned.
'I'm sorry, Zo—I really thought
that I could turn away, forget
the past, and not look back—' He's short
of breath; his slumping silhouette
is racked by pain at every syllable;
his voice is dampened—'But I can't.
My empty soul is not refillable
like this. It isn't that you aren't
attractive—wonderful—you are!
It's just that I can't go this far.'

2:36 am

'What is it—don't you find me sexy?'
asks Zoe. 'No—that isn't true!
Most guys would have an apoplexy
at just the merest glimpse of you—
I've seen it all, and though my mind
is blown away, I can't deny
that my true loyalty's confined
to someone else: the girl who I
split up with just this afternoon.
It's over, but I'm clearly fated
to be with no one else so soon—
I've been emotionally castrated,
and any substitutes are banned...
I don't expect you'll understand.'

2:39 am

'Not understand?' says Zoe. 'Give
me just a little credit, please.
You think it's possible to live
all these adventures overseas
without discovering a thing
or two about the human state?
No bluesman ever hoped to sing
of all the woes that complicate
the battlefield *I* call existence!
You fancy you're the first affair
to sour on me, through all this distance?
Your obstacles are hardly rare.
Don't fret for me, Glenn—I've befriended
too many fools to be offended.'

2:42 am

Glenn sits back down on Zoe's bed,
his elbows resting on his knees,
his face within his hands. 'Instead
of letting this romance appease
my aching heart, I've made it all—
despite intention—ten times worse,'
he sighs. 'Is this my fate—to fall
so low? In trying to immerse
my sorrows here, I've hurt us both:
cheapened myself, insulted you—
that's something I was always loath
to do to anyone. Review
tonight's debacle and you'll see
that there's no greater ass than me.'

2:45 am

Zo stands and paces through the room,
passing before the gauzy drapes
so that the moon and stars illume
her body with exotic shapes
against her pale and naked skin
a moment longer—then she slips
into a silk kimono, thin
and delicate, whose folds eclipse
the graceful contours of her form.
'Here, put this on,' she offers, throwing
a hotel dressing-gown of warm
material to Glenn. 'Quit showing
your naked body off like that,
and sit down here. We'll have a chat.'

2:48 am

A little tentatively, Glenn
obeys, and lets his body fall
beside her on the sofa. 'Men—
and teenage men!' she laughs. 'You're all
the same, you know—you're helpless fools
set loose upon a female world
with little knowledge of the rules
to keep yourselves from being hurled
headlong through permanent disaster.
You're out of touch with your emotions,
and ignorance makes fear your master.
You're unaccustomed to the notions
of self-acceptance, honesty
and trust—you're cripples, don't you see?'

2:51 am

'Thanks for the pepping up,' Glenn mutters:
'There goes my self-esteem.' 'Ah, ego—
the vainest, emptiest of strutters!'
she says: 'Machismo's no amigo
of yours—no, it's a curse, my friend:
an enemy you must defeat
at once, if ever you intend
to love again. It's obsolete.'
They sit in silence in the dark,
considering their common plight,
feeling it fruitless to embark
on further arguments tonight.
Glenn simply says, 'I thank you, Zo—
for everything. I have to go.'

2:54 am

Two figures sprawl upon the lawn
beneath the arbour's dappled shade,
decked in the costumes they were born
wearing, and willing to parade
their secrets in the silver light.
They sport two different tones of skin—
one ebony, the other white—
and curl in symbiosis, yin
and yang described within their ring
of bodies loosely intertwined.
They gaze above—at anything
and nothing—with a common mind
removed from simple neural tissue,
devoid of any pressing issue.

2:57 am

Rebecca is the first to stir.
She stretches, and emits a sound
of satisfaction. 'I'd prefer
to stay here, lying on the ground
for all my life, than ever think
of getting up,' she says. 'I'm so
relaxed that I'm about to sink
beneath the grass and far below,
until the very planet swallows
me deep into its core.' 'My arms
and legs have taken root,' Kris follows.
'This patch of dewy turf embalms
me whole, and I'm about to melt
into its lush, abundant pelt.'

3:00 am

They lie back in contentment, sharing
these images. 'Just think—this morning
I was an anguished soul, despairing
at what I had to do, at spawning
a legacy of pain and trouble,'
Rebecca reminisces. 'Now,
here in this warm and cosy bubble
of safety and protection, how
remote and distant does that seem!
My mind has been entirely blanked
of worries. We make quite a team,
you know—and if I haven't thanked
you most sincerely for your part
in this, then I've ignored my heart.'

3:03 am

'No need to thank me,' Kris assures.
'Sadly, I've only helped you borrow
an instant—no reprieve endures
forever. I leave town tomorrow;
we'll have no chance to re-create
this fond occasion. We'll be placed
back in the daily, tangled state
we've temporarily erased
from thought today; we'll have to deal
with all the things that we've forsaken.
The opportunity to feel
tonight's enchantment must be taken,
but come the morning, day-to-day
reality must have its way.'

3:06 am

They're startled by a cracking twig:
'Oh, shit,' Bec whispers. 'What was that?'
'It sounded like a frenzied pig
or sabre-fanged and feral cat
rampaging through the undergrowth,'
Kristin suggests: 'Or, even worse,
it may be that our time of sloth
has left us open to the curse
we hoped we'd put to rest—exposure
to that park ranger!' 'No!' Bec wails.
'I thought if we'd escaped disclosure
as long as this, our cooling trails
would be forever safely hidden
from foes unwanted and unbidden.'

3:09 am

Despite their garments being caught
by complicating twigs and sticks,
and errors ('This is much too short—
it must be yours!' 'Forget it—mix
and match for now; we'll sort it out
another time!') before too long
they're fully clothed—although some doubt
remains about what might be wrong-
way-round or inside-out. The clamour
of trampled forestry increases
in volume, and their heartbeats hammer—
the parting undergrowth releases
a rabid wolf upon their clearing,
snarling and drooling, ever nearing.

3:12 am

Rebecca screams. The hound of hell
affixes her with bloodshot eyes,
and parts incisors to expel
a blasting roar that terrifies
both of them as the creature stalks
balefully closer. Becca quakes
in abject terror as it walks
toward them, and her whisper shakes
with fear: 'I'm not a coward, but
enormous dogs give me the creeps!'
Kris gasps, 'Hang on—I know that mutt—'
just as the fiendish canine leaps
violently at their hiding place
and licks her roughly in the face.

3:15 am

'Get back here, dog!' commands a tree
as Arthur and his clan appear
out of its shadowed folds to see
Zen panting into Kristin's ear.
'Well, fancy seeing you!' he pours
exuberantly. 'Are you lost
again? Is this a friend of yours?
How did you happen to be tossed
into this unattractive thicket?
What are you doing here—just strolling?
Tossing a frisbee? Playing cricket?
My friends were harmlessly patrolling
these gardens—which we oft frequent—
when Zen here recognised your scent.'

3:18 am

'Don't say a thing,' Rebecca warns.
'They're only drunks. They'll go away.'
'No, don't be stupid,' Kristin scorns
her paranoia. 'It's okay—
I know these people; they're my friends.'
Art bows and lifts his hat to Bec,
says, 'Pleased to meet you,' and extends
a friendly hand for shaking. 'Check
my clothes for weapons, if you will,'
he offers. 'But I know you'll find
no instrument to wound or kill
your body, spirit, soul or mind—
unless, of course, you count the pox
that flourishes within my socks.'

3:21 am

Rebecca shoots a troubled glance
at Kris, who nods to reassure.
'All right,' she says. 'I'll take a chance
and—just for now—assume that you're
not the itinerant psychotic
assassins I can't help but think
of you as being.' 'These quixotic
protectors tore me from the brink
of death and ruin,' Kris maintains.
Bec, humbled, says, 'If that's the case,
I'm sorry my suspicious brains
should be so eager to embrace
so blindly prejudiced a view—
my name's Rebecca; who are you?'

3:24 am

A catalogue of introductions
ensues, and friendly affability
dismantles all of the obstructions
between Rebecca and civility;
before too long, they talk like friends
of old, as Will recites a verse
about a tree, and Rock defends
what he refers to as 'the curse
of thoroughbred, exalted man'.
Sporadically, Zen barks aloud,
and Eddie hands around a can
of which he is especially proud.
Kris tells of cities, and compares
their virtues; Bec just sits and stares.

3:27 am

'You're troubled,' Art evaluates
of Bec. 'You seem reserved, withdrawn—
as if pursued by evil fates
that haunt without relief.' 'I've worn
a cheerful countenance as long
as I've been able,' she admits.
'I've tried to stay detached, and strong
against the unrelenting blitz
my treacherous emotions launch
against me. But I'm getting weary,
and it's impossible to staunch
the flow of obstinately dreary
impressions that inform my thoughts—
so, yes, you're right. I'm out of sorts.'

3:30 am

'A matter of the heart, perhaps?'
he hazards, and Rebecca nods.
'I thought so. Of the handicaps
imposed upon us—set at odds
with happiness—I'd bet my pants
that love remains the most effective.
How cruel is fate, to make romance
so fundamental a directive,
when love is fraught with so much peril?
And yet it seems that everyone—
aristocratic, common, feral—
is subject to its glamours; none
escape the bittersweet embrace
endemic to the human race.

3:33 am

'But love would not infest the earth
so universally unless
something about it made it worth
the constant struggle and distress
encapsulated in the state.
Although it's hard to scale a hill,
the view from high aloft is great;
although skydiving's known to kill
with problematic parachutes,
the sheer emotion of complete
exhilaration constitutes
the greatest thrill you'll ever meet,
I'm told—created by the virtue
that safety and restraint desert you.

3:36 am

'Perhaps you want to be a sparrow
and safely hop along the ground,
where there exists no bow and arrow
to shoot you down, and where are found
no predators and ample food.
It's easier to walk than fly,
and if that represents your mood
then keep your eyes turned from the sky
and be content with what you know.
But my opinion would inveigle
you otherwise: soar high, not low;
don't be a sparrow, but an eagle,
and weather any likelihood
of evil for a greater good.'

3:39 am

'You sound just like my boyfriend,' Bec
dismisses, further adding: 'Ex,
that is. You'd think a motor wreck
would constitute the true apex
of pleasure and excitement, paying
no thought to all the shattered lives
and pain.' However, as she's saying
these words, a nagging doubt contrives
to bring her thesis to a halt;
she falters: 'Or I once thought so.
I'm not so sure—' 'That's not your fault,'
Art says: 'You simply have to know
the place where you'd most rather be.'
'I do.' Bec grins. 'Just wait and see.'

3:42 am

I can't believe I'm here at four
A.M. in front of this computer—
but I can't take it anymore,
writes Zoe. *Since the persecutor*
that binds my mind won't seem to go,
I'm left employing desperate measures
for any chance to overthrow
its grip and get on with the pleasures
of normal, workaday existence.
Because of this, this week's report
is engineered with the assistance
of writing mechanisms fraught
with deviations from the style
that I've preferred for quite a while.

3:45 am

Zo rises, and describes a circuit
around her room. She knows her onus—
and her commitment not to shirk it—
but it would surely be a bonus
if this odd city had presented
itself to her within a more
expedient disguise. Prevented
from playing to her standard score,
she plans a radical departure
from what she's long considered normal,
much like a regimental marcher
abandoning her strict and formal
procedure for a road unlined—
she hopes her editors won't mind.

3:48 am

The hotel room is fine, she writes.
The food is good; the weather, pleasant.
But during all the days and nights
for which I've been alert and present
within this city, it's been rare
to find the touristy attractions
that constitute the standard fare
of travel columns. My reaction's
been positive, and not unfavourable,
however. For upon my quest
to savour everything that's savourable
I've noticed that what I like best
is no museum, church with steeple
or monument—but, rather, people.

3:51 am

Without life, there can be no city.
No neatly-structured pile of stone,
cement and glass—however pretty—
could ever constitute alone
the sprawling catalogue of tales
that make a town a place to live.
A vibrant atmosphere prevails
wherever people meet, to give
a total greater than the sum
of all its parts. With this in mind,
although initially I'd come
traditionally disinclined
to venture past the concrete part,
since then I've had a change of heart.

3:54 am

I've met peculiar people here,
with individual obsessions
that could, perhaps, be viewed as queer,
evaluating first impressions.
People who value humble things—
from football codes to city grids—
who've weathered life's repeated stings—
losing their parents and their kids—
but haven't yet abandoned hope,
content to simply be alive,
and glad to resolutely grope
for any joy that may derive
from common, everyday affairs—
an admirable world is theirs.

3:57 am

This afternoon, I shared the soul
of someone who I'd never met
before. He took me to a hole
beneath a marble headstone, set
with private memories and moods
that filled its void to overflowing.
I spent repeated interludes
among the people coming, going,
stopping to show the briefest snatches
of what went on inside their heads—
and weaved together all these patches
into the most ornate of spreads:
a tapestry of joyous being,
a work of art—or life—worth seeing.

4:00 am

A simple story, one might say,
and one too dull to be repeated.
But what impressed me was the way
these unassuming, unconceited
townsmen and women were so quick
to open themselves up to me.
As soon as I acquired the trick
of unaffected empathy,
my foreign consciousness perceived
a trove of magic which, before
this education, I'd believed
to be a subject fit to bore
its sorry audience to tears—
how narrow, now, that view appears!

4:03 am

I guess this column's not about
a southern town called Adelaide,
but in the wonders found throughout
the world. Don't ever let them jade
upon you with their repetition.
Don't take for granted what you see
from day to day. The recognition
of beauty is the apogee
of sensory illumination;
to see such splendour all around
with genuine appreciation
is something that should not be drowned
in cynicism, dull and flat
and tedious. Remember that.

4:06 am

She reads this over, checks the spelling
and readjusts the punctuation.
To her, at least, it makes compelling
and captivating dissertation,
and if the world is too obtuse
to think the same, what can she do?
Next week she plans to introduce
an exposé of Uluru
and other sites near Alice Springs:
her editors will be relieved
that she's reverted to the things
they pay for, and she'll be reprieved
for unexpectedly revealing
the strange emotions she's been feeling.

4:09 am

She wonders vaguely where Glenn went,
but has a pretty good idea
of her Lothario's intent.
She thinks back on her night with cheer,
and saves her new report to disk,
carving her words upon the stone
of magic to avoid the risk
of their erasure. Lying prone
upon her bed, she pulls the cord
of her kimono and allows
the silk to fall away toward
the floor. She feels the night air douse
her body with its warmth; her sleep
is instantaneous and deep.

4:12 am

As Kristin lies upon her bunk,
she listens to the pleasant sound
of people sleeping. One is drunk
and snoring raggedly; spellbound
by dreams, some mumble random phrases
in foreign tongues; another slumbers
so silently that Kris appraises
no sign of life. These dormant numbers
appear no more than shadowed lumps
beneath their coloured sleeping bags—
as though the beds had sprouted humps
like camels—but their presence drags
a comforting response from Kris;
she sighs in safe, untroubled bliss.

4:15 am

For who could ever feel alone,
surrounded by the dozing forms
of others? Though she's never known—
at least in waking hours—the dorm's
inhabitants, she knows their kind,
for she is one. She feels united
with each of them: at home, combined
in comradeship. She's long delighted
to revel in the atmosphere
surrounding strangers lost in lands
as strange as any pioneer
discovered: each one understands
the others' plight; they cling together
against the world, the fates, the weather.

4:18 am

Along the way, she's left a trail
of friends, companions, kindred souls
and lovers, as a lonely snail
leaves tracks of silver on its strolls
around its garden universe,
material possessions perched
upon its back. The vagrant's curse
consists of having slowly searched
through every corner of the globe
to find a friend, then being forced
to say goodbye. No xenophobe
could be so bitterly divorced
from such an ever-winding string
of soulmates—it's a painful thing.

4:21 am

Tonight's impassioned introduction
is just another in a series
of friendships destined for destruction.
She's formulated many theories
of unavoidable assumptions
applied to such relationships—
but all to no avail. Her gumption's
too insubstantial to eclipse
her fundamental urge to bind
herself in passionate alliance
with any colleague she can find—
apparently in sheer defiance
of all the pain and inner wars
that her departures always cause.

4:24 am

But she's consoled to think that Bec,
at least, needs less of her attention.
The ragman's wisdom seemed to check
a storm of conflict and dissension
Kris hadn't even recognised
until it was alleviated.
Bec's glowing features symbolised
her fortune newly reinstated,
and, suddenly, she left to catch
a taxi home. Her rushed farewells—
fond as they were—could not dispatch
the vague confusion that still dwells
in Kristin's mind. *What's going on?*
she almost asked. But Bec was gone.

4:27 am

Attempting now to comprehend
Rebecca's sudden change of heart,
she feels her thoughts begin to bend
persistently away, to dart
through disentangling neural tracks
with little evidence of pattern
or plan. She feels her limbs relax
until her body seems to flatten
itself upon her bed and she's
no longer body, merely thought
passing along a mental frieze—
a self-imagined astronaut
in unpredictable terrain
within her boundless mind's domain.

4:30 am

'What foreign stars are sparkling here?'
she wonders. 'And what constellations
are drawn across this hemisphere
in new and alien formations?
A hidden hand has come to write
a story in a million stars,
a different chapter every night,
the blackened books of time's memoirs.
And here I am—I've lost the plot.
I've somehow started halfway through.
At least the moon retains its spot,
and pulses—new to full to new—
and leads me, like a constant friend,
and guides me, somehow, to the end.'

4:33 am

She knows that she's about to fall
asleep, but for a while enjoys
the fleeting and disjointed sprawl
of images her mind employs
to rid itself of conscious thought.
She reinvents the day's agenda,
letting her wearied brain distort
reality to aery splendour.
She knows that she'll be forced to leave
this place first thing tomorrow, lest
another day lets her perceive
the very same surroundings dressed
in drab and everyday attire,
much to her sorrow and her ire.

4:36 am

This topic brings her to reflect
on all the places that she's been;
on roaming unrestrained, unchecked
across an unrestricted scene.
She thinks of cities celebrated
in movies, where her feet have trod;
of chunks of history, undated
through all their weathered years; of Todd
and more successful coalitions.
She ponders home, left far behind
her all-consuming global missions—
the last thing passing through her mind
is that she hasn't mourned Denmark
since she began. Then all is dark.

4:39 am

Even those partying all night
along the dingy neon drag—
which constitutes the city's height
of merrymaking—start to flag
as DJs wearily announce
that closing time is drawing nigh
and monkeymen prepare to bounce
those revellers too drunk or high
on sundry uppers—artificial
or natural—to arrest their feasts
of excess: though they meet initial
resistance, these tuxedoed beasts
soon wrench an end to any doubt;
the street begins to empty out.

4:42 am

A flow of traffic is sustained
along the dying, littered strip.
Muscle cars full of young men trained
in etiquette adroitly quip
a wealth of artful witticism
(like, 'Get your gear off, sexy chicks!')
and give constructive criticism
to random passers-by ('You're pricks!').
Once-noble fops drift up the street,
their shirts unbuttoned, ties untied;
the nightclubs' pumping primal beat
is suddenly solemnified
into a grimly tolling bell
sounding the fading night's death knell.

4:45 am

Few people look at home along
this slice of alien terrain
frequented by a shifting throng
of ghosts and otherwise profane
itinerants. But one bold posse
parades along the pavement, showing
no deference to any bossy
demon or revenant, and flowing
in self-assured unstoppability.
They stride as if they rule the street,
and any question of humility
among this vagabond elite
will not be met with gratitude,
but likelier with angry feud.

4:48 am

'I love this time of night,' Art waxes.
'It's when the masses recognise
that all their governmental taxes
give them no right to exercise
their mythical prerogative
to walk our turf. They stay indoors
quite willingly, and where we live
is no more theirs, but mine and yours—
and that's the natural way of things.
When despots leave, our people rule
like once-exiled, returning kings,
and we don't have to play the fool
to foolish peasants anymore—
our powers rise excelsior!'

4:51 am

'And so—to life!' cries Eddie, handing
a multitude of empty tins
around their legion. 'Notwithstanding
the fact that these contain no gins—
or even tonics—let's propose
a toast upon this briefest night:
to vanquishing life's many foes,
to using wit to stymie might,
to having lived another day
with bodies, souls and minds intact;
to having cheery tunes to play—
and songs to sing—despite the fact
that we're still living on the street.
Can there be any greater feat?'

4:54 am

'None whatsoever,' Rocky chimes.
'No theatre, temple, gambling hall
or nightclub ever held such times
as we've enjoyed here. No deb ball
or private, black-tie dinner function
could see a crowd so well-esteemed
as us. Until a recent junction
within my life, I'd always dreamed
of being treated as an equal
in noble circles—I was blind.
Such falsity will have no sequel,
I promise—for I know I'll find
no greater happiness than that
within this urban habitat.'

4:57 am

'Well spoken,' Will congratulates.
'There's poetry in you, my friend.
It's plain this city cultivates
such wealths of culture as transcend
these seemingly banal surrounds—
I see no other explanation
for all the wonder that astounds
my newly-found appreciation
of these—so humble!—lives we lead.
We're poet, connoisseur, musician
and noble beast: why should we need
to modify this proud position?
For if there's nothing that we lack,
why waste our time in looking back?'

5:00 am

'You all sound like a bad commercial
on television,' Art chastises.
'It's really not that controversial.
It seems as though your speech comprises
raw sentiments to the effect
that everyone should quit their jobs,
forsake commodities, reject
suburban lives, and live like slobs
with us. "It's fun to do without—"
you clamour—"Poverty's a riot!"
Like just-converted and devout
fanatics, begging all to try it...
but would you really recommend
this destitution to a friend?

5:03 am

'I know that none of us fare badly,
but just try not to overdo it.
Though I'd not change my lifestyle gladly,
it isn't right to misconstrue it
as suitable for everyone.
There's sometimes pain, more often hunger—
and even death—among this "fun".
It's not my plan to play scaremonger,
but—think about a girl like Kris.
Although she's full of strength—assertive,
and unafraid of the abyss
of treachery that lingers, furtive,
through all the perils that occur—
I wouldn't wish this life on her.'

5:06 am

They're sobered by this contemplation,
and walk in silence for a spell,
engaged in thoughtful rumination
on heaven, purgatory and hell
on earth—and whether they're the same—
till Arthur yawns, and says, 'I'm beat.
It's almost dawn, and none could claim
this lengthy day's been incomplete
in terms of noble deeds fulfilled,
excitement, travel, magic—truly,
no dandy musketeering guild
could hope to muster such unruly
adventure as we've had today—
it's time to hit the sack, I'd say.'

5:09 am

A vacant warehouse block ensures
that for tonight, at least, they'll sleep
in partial shelter. Art secures
a half-sprung mattress; others heap
their clothes upon the ground to make
their makeshift beds. Rock whistles, lacking
his flute, and Ed lies, half-awake,
beneath an eiderdown of sacking.
Zen twitches, lost in canine dreams,
and Will observes the full moon shining
through broken skylights. Soon, the team's
adrift in sleep, their snores combining
in harmony, and only Art
remains attentively apart.

5:12 am

He looks around the spartan cell,
and speculates that life is fine.
Today, at least—for who can tell
what obstacles lie down the line,
or what the fates decide tomorrow?
Who knows which of the seeds of time
will grow, and which will not—to borrow
from Shakespeare? Gladly, Arthur's prime
concern is not with such remote
eventualities, but stays
away from that far asymptote
the future: individual days
of happiness are all he asks
from karma's tragicomic masks.

5:15 am

They say tomorrow never comes;
the future never will exist;
the past amounts to scattered crumbs
of nothing, which will not be missed.
The present is the only solid
reality: the moment—fleeting,
ephemeral, however squalid,
superb or glorious, retreating
into the distance at the speed
of time—is all that ever matters.
To chase its trails as they recede
impossibly—to clutch at tatters
of past dissolving—is to waste
the present times not yet erased.

5:18 am

So Arthur revels in the sliver
of time that he's been granted, glad
that fate's consented to deliver
another slice of present clad
in cheerful and untroubled garb.
The silent darkness floods his mind
with easy peace, and dulls the barb
of injuries left far behind
in memory and time. Surrounded
by friends, sensations oddly numb,
suspicion and distrust confounded
by warmth, he feels himself succumb
to dark oblivion's request.
His head drops slowly to his chest.

5:21 am

It's darkest just before the dawn,
but moonlight casts the quarry floor
with nets of silver that adorn
each surface with a secret store
of gleaming half-light. Shadowed trees
and rocks build strange and eerie shapes
against the skyline—vortices
darker than darkness as they traipse
along the edges of the night.
The quarry towers high aloft,
appearing infinite in height,
its rocky outcrops blurred and soft
in outline, seeming to extend
in all directions without end.

5:24 am

The tumbled rocks still radiate
the merest hint of warmth, supplied
by sunlight stored within the slate
and sandstone statues that reside
around the quarry. Daytime's ghost
aside, the scene does not resemble
the crucible presented *post*
meridien, which saw rocks tremble
and undulate behind the haze
of searing heat. Instead, the air
is still and softened, and the day's
assault has ceased to overbear,
and is itself subdued; respite
now rules beneath the gaze of night.

5:27 am

The Eagle Rock seems even more
impressive as its shadowed crags
loom mightily above to claw
the heavens with their outstretched jags.
It seems to overlook the world:
the street lamps' neon spiderweb;
the strip of ocean, darkly pearled
with starlight flowing with the ebb
of wave and tide; the distant hills
that watch the town like tireless guards;
the constant stream of life that mills
around the streets, the houses, yards,
casualties of suburban sprawl—
the Eagle watches over all.

5:30 am

From this unequalled vantage-point,
Glenn oversees the world below.
Perched on the Eagle's neck—conjoint
in spirit, so they see and know
from one omniscient perspective—
he sits as one who plans to sit
forever, locked in one reflective
position till the planets quit
rotating and the universe
grinds slowly to a final halt;
content to let his mind immerse—
though freshly wounded—into salt
time and again, to feel the sting
these self-inflicted tortures bring.

5:33 am

His memory's in overdrive,
producing eerie, fleeting flashes
of recollection that contrive
to spur him onward as he dashes
his head against a ghostly wall.
He smells the scent of perfume, hears
a silent, spectral chorus call
his name—and as this disappears,
he feels the texture of soft skin,
a micron from his fingertips—
too far to touch—and tastes a grin
playing across expectant lips.
He senses these, yet cannot see:
the phantoms of an amputee.

5:36 am

An apparition that asserts
itself more strongly than the rest
for one brief moment disconcerts
his vigil. Noises manifest
themselves within the undergrowth
below: a leafy tree branch rustles,
a twig is cracked, a muttered oath
is faintly heard. Glenn feels his muscles
contract in tension, whirls around
and scans the panorama spread
below him—though he knows the sound
doesn't exist outside his head.
The world seems only a mutation
of his deranged imagination.

5:39 am

But here, at least, a concrete thing
appears: a ghost that he can see,
and touch, and feel, and grasp, and cling
onto for life and sanity.
A legend carved upon the rock—
as tangible as stone itself,
near powerful enough to knock
him senseless from the rugged shelf—
emerges from the fading night,
asserting that 'Glenn loves Rebecca'.
He lifts a stone with all his might,
to heft it at this fraud, this wrecker
of lives, progenitor of hate—
until a voice cries, 'No, Glenn—wait!'

5:42 am

He turns; another apparition
is climbing to the Eagle's summit.
He's seized by sudden recognition;
he drops his stone, half-hears it plummet
to rocky death, and cries, 'That you?
Are you for real? Or did I make
you up? I'm going crazy—who
or what goes there? I just can't take
this anymore!' He cracks his knees
against the rock, and limply slumps,
as if a sudden bone disease
had struck him. Fighting with the lumps
that clog his throat, he blocks his eyes
with desperate fists, and softly cries.

5:45 am

But when he takes away his hands
the spectre hasn't disappeared
compliantly, but firmly stands
above him, saying: 'God! I feared
I'd find you here in such a state.
Have you been drinking? You look awful.'
Confused, Glenn mutters, 'No—I'm straight.
Just sitting here; is that unlawful?'
'I guess not,' answers Bec. 'There room
for me as well?' Glenn just nods mutely,
leaving Rebecca to resume
haltingly. 'This is absolutely
the final place I thought I'd find
myself,' she says. 'But never mind...'

5:48 am

'What are you doing here?' Glenn asks.
'I thought that you'd—' 'This has to rate
among the very hardest tasks
I've ever had to contemplate,'
Bec interrupts. 'If you could know
what I've been going through these last
few hours—and days—you might forego
my friendship, thinking that I've passed
the line of rational lucidity
and live in lunatic psychosis.'
Glenn says, 'Enough of this stupidity—
that wouldn't be my diagnosis
at all—unless evaluating
what's lately been *my* madness-rating.'

5:51 am

'You too?' Rebecca laughs. 'We make
the perfect couple. Can we book
a double padded room?' 'I'd take
that up without a second look—
or thought,' Glenn says. 'But tell me—what
exactly has been going on
since this time yesterday?' 'It's not
important, Glenn—I've undergone
a lot of crazy mental changes
of late, but here's the bottom line:
no matter how fate rearranges
its elements, I won't resign
myself to live in doubt and fear—
I'll stand strong, and I'll stay right here.'

5:54 am

She leans her head against his shoulder;
he wraps an arm around her waist.
Sitting atop the jagged boulder
that is the Eagle Rock, displaced
by time and distance from their lives
outside, all they can do is bask
in the contentment that derives
from contact. They don't need to ask
what fate tomorrow morning brings;
they know tonight will last forever,
immune from time's evasive wings.
And if it doesn't—as it never
can hope to do—it doesn't matter.
The former always rules the latter.

5:57 am

It's early: coming up to six,
to be exact. The skyline's glowing
towards the east as sunlight licks
the far horizon, almost showing.
Today will be a fraction shorter
than yesterday: midsummer's passed
across the sleeping earth like water
beneath a bridge. But for the cast
of solstice's phantasmagoria,
a day can live beyond its hours—
the pain and pleasure—fear, euphoria—
don't fade, for they have lasting powers
forever growing and extending—
no story ever has an ending.

COPYRIGHT

First published in 1994 by Allen & Unwin.

This edition published in 2021 by Ligature Pty Limited
34 Campbell St · Balmain NSW 2041 · Australia
www.ligatu.re · mail@ligatu.re

e-book ISBN: 9781922730336

ligature untapped

This print edition published in collaboration with Brio Books, an imprint of Booktopia Group Ltd

Level 6, 1A Homebush Bay Drive · Rhodes NSW 2138 · Australia

Print ISBN: 9781761281716

briobooks.com.au

The paper in this book is FSC® certified. FSC® promotes environmentally responsible, socially beneficial and economically viable management of the world's forests.